PLAYWRITING
in
PROCESS

PLAYWRITING
in
PROCESS

Thinking and Working Theatrically

Michael Wright

HEINEMANN
PORTSMOUTH, NH

Heinemann
A division of Reed Elsevier Inc.
361 Hanover Street
Portsmouth, NH 03801-3912
Offices and agents throughout the world

Library of Congress Cataloging-in-Publication Data
Wright, Michael.
Playwriting in process: thinking and working theatrically / Michael Wright.
p. cm.
Includes index.
ISBN 0-435-07034-7
1. Playwriting. I. Title.
PN1661.W75 1997
808.2—dc21
97-1815
CIP

Acquisitions Editor: Lisa A. Barnett
Production Editor: Renée Nicholls
Cover Designer: Renée Nicholls
Manufacturing Coordinator: Louise Richardson

Printed in the United States of America on acid-free paper
01 00 99 98 97   DA   1 2 3 4 5

For my Dad,
John Wright,
the original great storyteller,
and for
Ben Herman,
the first one to say,
"You're a writer."

CONTENTS

ACKNOWLEDGMENTS

SPECIAL THANKS GO TO DAVID COHEN, GARY GARRISON, Harlene Marley, and Jeffrey Sweet for their encouragement and support. Lisa Barnett, the editor of this book, deserves kudos for her astute comments and guidance, and for such patience, vision, and class. I also wish to thank the students who have taught me so much, Elena Carrillo, Lisa D'Amour, and chief among them, Clay Nichols. I can only hope this book shows my gratitude sufficiently. To the People Playhouse folks in New Orleans, and the New York Writers' Bloc members I want to say thanks for the roots. Finally, my family—Judy, Hannah, and Eli—deserves special credit for putting up with the muttering hermit in the other room and for brightening up my life every day.

INTRODUCTION

THE URGE THAT LED TO THIS BOOK CAME FROM THE FRUSTRA-
tions many of my colleagues around the country share with playwriting textbooks that aren't generally very useful in the classroom.
I decided I wanted a broad compendium of exercises that could be
assigned to students with varying needs and levels, something students would carry with them beyond the classroom in much the
same way that directing students hang on to Viola Spolin's monu-
mentally important *Improvisation for the Theatre*.

The intent of my book is to reach beyond the needs of the student playwright as well. The exercises can be done on a rudimenta-
ry or sophisticated level and can be put together in a virtually
infinite number of combinations to explore craft and ideas in any
direction a playwright wishes.

Playwriting in Process is intended to act as a resource, a craft
reminder and reinforcer, a stimulus, a self-teaching mechanism,
and a reference work. As a result, this book does not follow any kind
of formulaic approach to the making of a play. It's my belief that formulas impose an inhibitive sense of style and limited theatrical
thinking on a writer. My suggestion to all who express a sincere
interest in pursuing the craft has always been to "read a million
plays, and see twice that many."

This suggestion may sound a bit flip, but there is no longer any
meaningful single definition of a play that applies across the spectrum of what's being created around the world, beyond saying that

a play is a (largely) live event that takes place in a space that all involved have agreed is a "stage." In the first two chapters, the basic concept or perspective of what makes a play a play is examined through the terms "thinking theatrically" and "working theatrically." This perspective underlies all the exercises that follow in the book.

There are some who insist that any book that attempts to discuss playwriting must be chock-full of definitions and examples from famous plays. I think examples from famous plays tend to frustrate beginning playwrights and annoy experienced ones. It is my contention that playwrights make their own definitions from trial and error. Playwriting is an *art* even though we refer to it as a craft; the latter implies that playwrights simply become apprenticed and five years later have achieved playwright status. Almost anyone can learn the rudiments, but learning how to release (if not unchain) the spirits for a unique work of art only comes from making plays over and over again.

Watching master playwrights struggle with their latest plays would be a great training ground. We could learn by watching how they make decisions about plot, which structure to place the plot in, how late to get into the action of the play, and how much needs to be known about their characters. Since the chance to watch such processes is extremely limited, the alternative is to watch yourself in the same struggles. In fact, the guiding principle of *Playwriting in Process* is for writers to become their own masters. In doing these exercises, you can provide yourself with examples of what will and what won't work according to individual taste and the play being worked on at the time.

Which brings me back to my argument about providing examples from famous plays. Reading work that already exists is dealing only with a product and not a process; furthermore, simply reading one example from a whole piece is the equivalent of seeing just the highlights of a sporting event. If you are to learn from and understand the importance of the home run, field goal, or slam dunk, you must understand its context. My choice of a wonderful example of dialogue is based on my view of dialogue as I have developed it over the years—I'd much rather that students find their own examples of great dialogue or, better yet, create their own examples. There are a number of suggestions in the book of plays to read to form a reference point to a given topic of discussion but these suggestions should encourage readers to consider the whole context of a work they choose.

I'd also argue that I couldn't just show one selection of dialogue because there are literally hundreds of choices that will show various points, whose importance depends on context. If I show how Marsha Norman brilliantly reveals a husband and wife's garbled communication in her play *Trudy Blue* during a conversation about going out for dinner, I'd have to show how Arthur Miller does the same thing in *All My Sons* when Kate Keller forgets to keep the lie going in just one word and sets the play sliding irrevocably toward its end. I'd have to show how one word can be a play's fulcrum, while one exchange may not have major dramatic results but can set the stakes for later events. Then I'd want to show numerous examples of what dialogue can do. But when I was done I would have still not covered the possibilities that students would discover on their own from both "reading a million plays" and through the actual hands-on work of doing the exercises.

Another approach in my playwriting books is to show samples of "successful" exercises. Again, this creates an imposition that tends to inhibit creativity. Human nature is to copy what we don't know how to do, and so a student ends up putting together a xerox of what the sample looks like. But where does the student go from there? The point of these exercises is to have the experience of doing, not of copying or finishing.

So much for what the book is not and what you won't find in it. What you will encounter in this book is a series of exercises, all grouped by their application to certain aspects of playwriting such as character and plot. In each exercise there is a discussion of what I intend to help the writer discover and some additional discussion on theatrical thinking and working. Each exercise allows the student to try a certain aspect of writing for the stage while helping to focus the process of that writing and its impact on the stage. Most exercises are cross-referenced to other exercises in the book that will encourage you to look at another angle on the same process.

As we progress to the end of the decade, century, millennium, and beyond, there is little reason to believe that theatre will retreat to the well-made play or to some rigid Aristotelian framework. Theatre is far more likely to continue its expansion of form, subject matter, language, use of space, and so on. In fact, it will continue to embrace its eclectic heritage from the experimenters of the twentieth century. *Playwriting in Process* attempts to address this expansion by defining the essentials of theatrical thinking and working and presents exercises for playwrights at any level to fashion their own definitions, processes, and choices.

In spite or because of the oppressive mentality prevalent in America in this time period with regard to the arts, theatre continues to evolve in an open and free manner. Let's hope that our students, peers, colleagues, master practitioners, and teachers do the same.

CHAPTER

Thinking Theatrically

ONE OF THE MOST INTERESTING TEACHING CHALLENGES I'VE experienced is dealing with a student population that does not innately think "theatrically." I find that most of my students tend to think in terms of film, television, or print fiction writing—which makes sense since those varieties are their biggest influences. However much I may understand these influences, it doesn't resolve the dilemma. When a student writes a one-act play that calls for twenty different realistically rendered locations with a cast of a hundred or has every character self-narrate their exposition, motivation, and actions, I know that this student understands neither the realities nor the potential of the stage.

Even worse, when I evaluate scripts by "professionals" and find the same basic lack of understanding, I realize we have a problem that may be of epidemic proportions. So how do we fix this problem?

One obvious solution is to have the students read more plays, but even that has not been entirely satisfactory. The students tend to do what all artists do at first and mirror their influences. In other words, when I teach Williams, I get dark, poetic dramas back from my students. To solve this problem I've selected as wide a range of styles as I can, but the mirroring still goes on. While I don't see mirroring itself as necessarily bad, I am concerned that the students usually have no idea of the dramaturgical basis for the style they're aping—we can look at the product, but there's virtually no way to understand how the playwright arrived at that product.

One response is to have the students write as much as possible, so that they encounter firsthand the struggles endemic to making a play. Such writing encourages them to focus on their own experiences, values, and voices—to encourage absolutely original work. In this instance, they often find solutions to stage problems that are unique and highly imaginative.

But even in the best situations, another layer of this problem remains: rewriting. How do they go about correcting what's wrong with their plays? In my classes, we do detailed oral and written critiques of the pieces as they are developing, whether students are working on five-minute "get-in-late, get-out-early" pieces or one-act plays. When we say to one student that her plot is working reasonably well but we have no idea what the main character is all about, how should she go about creatively responding to that observation? How do you make a character more "real" or more complex or explore the range of reactions to a given situation to find the best solution?

I've read a great number of books on playwriting and screenwriting and most tend to say, "Do it this way," as if there are standard formulas. While I don't wish to denigrate anyone else's approach to playwriting none of these books has ever succeeded for me. Not one has satisfied the two problems I've identified here: how do we learn to think theatrically, and how do we learn to work theatrically on the problems of writing for the theatre?

As playwrights, I believe we need to start by considering the components of the theatrical and end by trying to access and utilize these components in our writing. Consider the theatre place itself: the stage. What is a stage? Taken at its most literal, a stage is usually a somewhat elevated, dusty floor that is somehow bordered by seats. There are usually lights, and sometimes curtains, and/or a proscenium arch. When there's a show on this stage, there's a set of some kind, and actors move around on this floor according to the needs of the play. But, whether there's a show mounted on it or not, a stage is always a physical representation of potential. The stage is a space that contains possibilities, not realities: it is a place for imagining.

For that reason, a blank stage is one of the most interesting things around. I can sit in an empty auditorium and look at a blank stage and conjure the endless possibilities for that space, from *Oedipus* to *Angels in America* and beyond. As a regional playwriting representative for the Kennedy Center/American College Theatre Festival, I travel throughout the year and see exactly such potential realized at the festivals I attend: day after day a given stage is converted from one world to another, going from a matinee of *True West* to an evening production of *Amadeus*.

In itself, then, a stage is theatrical. Even empty, it's a kind of show because the imagination is engaged by it. In use, there's no limit to what can happen there, unless the imagination itself is limited.

For instance, if you wanted to use a given stage but had no money for props, costumes, or lights, could you still do a show? Of course: props, costumes, and lights can be borrowed or made from found stuff. But could you still do a show without a stage?

Absolutely. We may be living in an era in which spectacle has taken over much of the commercial theatre, but the realm of the imagination continues all around us. Performance artists, new vaudevillians, and avant-garde theatre practitioners all utilize found spaces and alternative approaches to sets and costumes. And children's theatre, which is the easiest to discuss, has almost always relied on a less-is-more approach.

In good children's theatre, the emphasis is always on encouraging the audience to join in with the work rather than forcing the audience to watch passively. For example, an audience of children is quite happy with the idea of a plain chair representing a car. This same chair can be made to represent a throne, a mountain top, and a spaceship all in one show, and the audience can go along with these permutations quite agreeably. Further, since children's theatre needs to reach its population in a variety of venues, shows are successfully done in auditoriums, gyms, libraries, classrooms, parks, and parking lots—all because children are so willing to activate their imaginations.

Theatre for older children, who are sometimes referred to as adults, can do and already does the same thing, though we just tend not to think about it. After all, when you see a play, some part of you knows that the walls are made of painted fabric and that the actors are people with kids and mortgages just like yourself, but you make a contract with the stage and its event—the play—to ignore all that and put it aside.

This putting aside is usually described by one of the oddest phrases I've ever heard: the "willful suspension of disbelief." The phrase is quite accurate in what it describes but seems needlessly convoluted. I prefer the term "agreement," which just means that everything is in accord. If the play is set in Ireland, the actors learn Irish accents and agree among themselves that they're in a room in an old house in Dublin, and the audience says it will agree to go along with this as long as the actors don't do anything to make it stop, such as displaying a really poor accent. This example is a gross simplification of course, but what it means is that the stage can be anything provided the agreement is there.

Given that, the student I referred to earlier could write his one-act play with twenty locations and a hundred characters and make it work if he knew how to use the imaginative resources of the stage. His play could also be performed by one actor with one chair on a street corner, provided the script was written to create that agreement.

You could argue, of course, that an interpreter—a director or designer—could take the play as originally written and make a simplified, theatricalized version—imposing agreement. But my concern is with the connection made by playwrights to that theatrical concept on their own terms rather than relying on some future interpreter to do the work for the play. My experience has been that some directors guide your work well and some derail it. If you have thought ahead to the most imaginative concepts for your script, your chances of bringing play and audience into agreement are far better. In other words, you start and end by thinking theatrically.

One way of starting this process is by using the incredible advantages of the stage to connect with the imagination of the audience. This means that certain axioms of the theatre hold true, such as "suggest rather than spell out," and "show, don't tell."

Before defining those two concepts, let me provide a point of view for thinking about them: I try to encourage my students to think of watching a play as being involved in a mystery no matter what the style or subject matter of the play may be. The audience is there to figure out what's going to happen (in conventional theatre) because they're rooting for a particular character. We want Joe or Jane to fall in love, win the race, or outwit the Urban Slime Monster—but will they? What makes seeing a play fun is this very condition of not knowing what's going to happen while hoping things will go a certain way.

When something is spelled out, or told directly to us, it simply becomes less fun because our participation is denied. Imagine being told just before a game starts that "your team will lose by one point on a missed shot with one second left in the game."

The concepts "suggest rather than spell out" and "show, don't tell" are about giving the audience the chance to try to figure things out for themselves, of sustaining its agreement by actively engaging its imagination. To suggest means allowing an audience to draw its own conclusions from hints. If we watch a scene of a marriage ceremony, for example, and see the groom waiting nervously, and watch a very pregnant bride coming down the aisle to him, we naturally infer that the groom is probably the father of the child the bride will eventually deliver. We put two facts together to arrive at a third fact.

The example I just gave also applies to "show, don't tell," but we have to go a bit further to clarify this aspect because it's the one that truly separates theatre from other art forms.

A play is made up of a lot of different components, but two of the most important are the dialogue and the behavior of the characters. Dialogue is a complex thing. It includes what is said, what's meant by what is said, how it's said, and also what is not said.

Start with the text "I'm fine." What can be meant by the text is subtext, the attitude behind the words. For example, I can ask three different people how they are and get three entirely different answers with the same words simply by how they use those words to express their feelings. Joe might grit his teeth, annoyed to distraction by being asked the same stupid question once again, and he will spit the words out in a way that makes "I'm fine" sound more like "Go to hell." Sara, on the other hand, might be thrilled that someone wants to know how she is and sing the words out happily. James, who is depressed, might just mumble them.

The other option—what's not said—leads us back up to the notion of suggestion. If character A is called "immature, phony, and short" by character B, and character A responds by saying "I am not short!" we are inclined to understand that she accepts, in some way, the other two qualities. Much can also be "said" by silence or pauses. If one character simply does not respond to a statement, we infer certain things from this; if the same character pauses before responding, we tend to infer somewhat different things. What's not said has its own kind of subtext that makes the audience work a bit harder. The essence of good dialogue is allowing the fewest words to say or imply the most, or—as with silence or pauses—to allow the audience to infer the most. Which leads us to behavior.

Behavior is activity which reveals inner process. It may be what occurs in a pause or a silence, or it may be what occurs beyond the confines of dialogue. The playwright can show a tremendous amount about the character without having to use language. Virtually all plays contain stage directions such as "X walks to the door, and opens it to admit Y." This activity is necessary to the play because Y has knocked and can't get in unless X opens up. But activity alone does not tell us a great deal about a character. If X walks to the door and picks up a cream pie on the way to hit Y in the face, then we have behavior because we can read something in X's actions that tells us about her thoughts. There are also a hundred ways to write the quality of X's actual walk to the door, even without a pie: if she walks heavily, we infer one thing; if she runs to the door on tippytoes, we infer quite another. Behavior is obviously very important to the idea of "show, don't tell"—it spares us having to make character X say, "Well, I'll answer this door but I won't do it very gladly because it has got to be Y and I owe him a lot of money." The stage directions, then, create another kind of dialogue through behavior. And behavior is an extremely important aspect of thinking theatrically.

When a playwright uses behavior, he is recognizing a crucial element of theatre in the actions of a human being beyond words that define and move the story along. And this is because we must always remember that a play is a human event that is being observed by other humans—it is witnessed, in other words.

I define a play in production as a "witnessed present." This definition means all kinds of things. First, that any play we watch seems to happen now, whether it was written today or in 504 B.C., because the problems of the characters are being worked out in front of us, right here and now. And since the play needs this "us" in order to exist, it's our present at the same instant, because the problems of the characters reflect on our own lives. We may not have the literal dilemmas that Oedipus struggles with but we all have to deal with issues of morality and personal integrity on a daily basis. However, we can go further, because the entire gestalt of the play is a present event—a play needs real time in which to occur and is put on by real people in front of other real people. Humans are watching humans.

The moving images on a TV or film screen are reproductions; the people in the film scene we're watching are not doing that scene now. In fact, they may be at home, watching themselves at the same moment we are. But when we watch a play, the people performing in the play are right there; we are aware of them and they of us. And this means that thinking theatrically is also rooted in this aware-ness of the existence of the other.

We all like to watch people; it's a natural, human quality. We sit in airports, malls, and parks and watch the doings of others. And we understand far more from this kind of observation than we realize. For example, we know without hearing a word that the couple over there is arguing, or the man sitting to our left is really nervous. We read these things in the behavior of the people, but we also feel these things because we are in the same environment. When I lived in New York, I rode the subways nearly every day. A crowd of strangers, totally oblivious to one another, would become an elec-trified and connected group instantly if somebody abnormal or scary got on the train. Without any effort to communicate, we would all know to watch out and be careful: this person is sending out hos-tile or crazy energy. If that person subsequently left the car, you would immediately feel the flood of relief all around you, and some-times there would even be eye contact between passengers (usual-ly *verboten* on subways), accompanied by smiles or those ironic headshakes that make life in New York bearable.

When we're in a theatre, we are focused by a successful show by the same kind of immediacy one experiences on the subway. There is no filter between you and what's acting on your sensory receptors: we listen, watch, and feel the human struggles on the stage directly.

Thinking theatrically means playwriting with those values in mind. Writing dialogue is not just spinning out a lot of clever words but crafting language that expresses both in text and subtext the deep inner feelings of the characters. Creating revealing behavior allows us to witness the struggle with those feelings. Using the space of the stage in the most imaginative ways possible engages the audience emotionally, intellectually, and viscerally. All of these serve to connect humans to human experiences.

The stage, to return to our starting point, is a place that is a physical representation of potential. It is, in more traditional terms, metaphoric. It can represent not only other places—Thebes, Elsinore, Mars—but other levels of being. This is another aspect of thinking theatrically: a person on a stage is larger than life just because of being on that stage, and so, therefore, is that person's character and humanity.

Characters in plays don't just have bad days, they have horrible, overwhelming days. Characters in plays aren't just people, they have personalities equivalent to the Macy's Thanksgiving Day Parade balloons. Oedipus, Juliet, Blanche DuBois, and Prior Walter are extremely complex people caught up in difficulties most of us never have to face. While television has become the province of average Americans caught-in-a-terrible-dilemma and film has followed suit and created one-dimensional heroes of impossible qualities, theatre has largely remained the place where the range of genuinely human qualities can be examined in a careful and caring way.

For example, I try to remind my students that our admiration for *Hamlet* is certainly warranted because of Shakespeare's incredible writing abilities, but that we must never forget that the play is the story of a college student caught up in a terrible conflict. Should he take revenge for his father's murder or not? The tabloid version might be that he's a rich kid from a recently broken home who would just like to forget the whole thing, go back to school, and hit the bars with his buddies. But because Shakespeare wrote about a conflicted personality so brilliantly and made his humanity so profound, he is far more than just a schoolboy with problems: he is a young person who has too great a problem to solve alone, who has nowhere to turn for help, who is a walking contradiction—maybe really crazy—and who we must watch in his struggle.

While the struggle is important, what's equally important is our feelings. We are in a room with someone suffering and we can't do anything about it. The stage is a powerful place of humanity, and the "witnessed present" keeps us totally focused on that humanity because it is the characters' humanity and our own, all in the same place and time.

What Shakespeare knew is that the humanity of Hamlet is more important than the story of Hamlet, which is why our young prince is by turns funny, cruel, cunning, savage, and childish. You can analyze the poetry and meaning of the play all you like, but to me the truly enduring quality of the work is the vividness of its main character. Hamlet is larger than life and so frustratingly human—he is theatrical.

The question that plagues all playwrights is how do we craft stories and people who are truly theatrical? How can we use the real potential of the space we call a stage? Remember that the playwright is the only creative artist in the naturalistic theatre. All the other artists interpret your work. The more you know about the work of those interpretive artists, the better.

For instance, Shakespeare was an actor. He knew what it was like to be on the stage and to contend with an audience. Does this mean that you should have some acting experience? Yes, it really does. Nothing will give you a quicker fix on the reality of the stage and on the realities of the people who will play your characters than trying it yourself in a class or in a show. (I believe wholeheartedly as well that student actors should try to playwrite, student directors should hang lights, and technical students should act.) At bare minimum you should get together with friends and read plays aloud, and act out the roles in your living room—again, just to get a sense of things.

What about directing? Staying with our man of the moment, Shakespeare was probably responsible for staging some of his plays (he lived in an era long before there was anyone officially designated as "director"). Does this mean you should do the same? Well, here I have to fudge a little: I would not generally advise directing your own play in a full production unless that play had been thoroughly workshopped and developed first. Most of my experience has been that having the other eye of the director (and in some cases, the additional eye of a dramaturg) can be extremely helpful simply because the playwright can remain focused on the writing problems and leave the solving of stage problems to others.

On the other hand, I have directed my own plays and found these productions to be excellent learning experiences, so I leave it to you to discover your own perspective on this matter. I can recommend directing plays other than your own. Again, even if it's just in your living room, the issue is that you have to approach a play quite differently as a director than you would as an actor, and all of these experiences will deeply inform your playwriting sensibilities.

If you know how actors or directors work, you will know how to craft your plays with an awareness of their arts that will greatly enhance your own. I would further suggest that you learn about set, costume, and light design. A writer who knows how visual artists work will recognize what their art forms can add to his own. More importantly, however, a knowledge of these areas will help you to think theatrically because you will have a deeper awareness of the capabilities of the environment you're writing for. How much set is really needed? Can a character's personality be expressed better by one key element of a costume rather than a full head-to-toe treatment?

These kinds of questions (and their solutions) will ultimately give the writer 1000 percent more control of his imaginative product, the script. I wouldn't say control in the production because that's another thing altogether, but anything you can do to aim your script at the production you hope for will be helpful. Also, your script choices are metaphorical choices, and the more you know about using the tools of the physical theatre to enhance your metaphorical range, the better.

By way of example, look at a play by Donald Margulies called *The Model Apartment*. In this play, Margulies wanted to make a point about survivors who have inflicted their sufferings from the Holocaust, including the death of a child, on the next generation.

Rather than have the point made on a sheerly verbal level, Margulies chose instead to put the two daughters—the living one called Debbie and the dead one called Deborah—on stage and have them played by the same actress. In order to distinguish between the two and to make a stronger point, Debbie is played in what's known as a "fat suit," which is a padded garment worn under the clothes to create the illusion of being overweight, while Deborah is played in an unpadded costume. Thus, we have the symbol of the survivors wanting the live daughter to be the rebirth of the dead one, plus the symbol of the massive guilt laid upon this living daughter in the form of the physical mass she carries around. This use of costuming—combined with other elements such as the set's real and not-real qualities—elevates the play from what might have been a moderately affecting reality to a powerful theatricality.

Margulies has made theatre from a theatrical point of view. Theatre is collaborative by nature, and the more each collaborator knows about the other area, the better the communication and the better the art. The more the playwright knows about the entire range of choices available, the more effective his expression can become.

Thinking theatrically has one final, crucial aspect: expressing your imaginative impulses. One of my students wrote a one-act in which two men compete for the same woman. In this script he has a character onstage named Love who walks around wearing a red, heart-shaped suit and who spouts poetry. Another student wrote a very allegorical piece in which characters appear with animal heads. Yet another wrote a short play in which a modern suitor has to pose as Sir Walter Raleigh to ask for permission to marry a woman whose institutionalized father believes he's Henry VIII. All of these plays represent an understanding that the stage is the place where any- and everything are possible and that using highly imaginative situations and characters triggers something magical in our brains.

This book was not written strictly for practitioners of naturalistic the-atre, although the majority of examples and ideas will be expressed in that form. In the past few decades, theatre artists have worked hard to blur the lines between theatre and other art forms, both to enhance the expressive capacity of theatre and to challenge the range of the modes they've borrowed from. Experimentation is to the benefit of all the arts and ought to be pursued more. (I see no reason, for example, why painting or sculpture majors don't take stage design or lighting, or even seemingly unrelated classes like acting or playwriting; it would only increase their perspective, and I know theatre people would grow tremendously by studying other artforms.)

Not enough experimentation is encouraged in theatre. Most of the schools I've come in contact with tend to stress realistic values in their main-stage work and relegate anything which is avant-garde or experimental to their studio theatres. Worse, the tendency is to put student-written work in the same backroom venues. I don't see how we can keep theatre vital if this continues to be our practice.

So, in closing this chapter, I would be remiss if I did not stress how compellingly theatrical most experimental work is. It constantly seeks to redefine the stage and the relationship between actor and audience. And it also succeeds or fails at the highest possible level because it is all about risk and the attempt to move another step closer to making the theatrical experience as artistically pure as possible.

I don't know what we can do about institutional thinking, but I know that individuals can open their minds. To that end, I would hope that anyone working from this book would do all of several things. First, become more familiar with theatre that is out of the mainstream by reading it, reading about it, seeing it, and becoming involved in it. Second, help out by bringing other people into contact with it. Thirdly and most importantly, seek to create your own vision on the stage, no matter what it takes to realize that vision. After all, unless you are in the theatre strictly for the money—which makes you either completely misguided or one of the most optimistic people on the planet—your work will always be truly original, experimental, and something never seen before.

Finally, then, I want to stress my belief that the techniques in this book will work for any kind of theatrical form, whether you want to reinvent the Greek tragedy or write a piece set in a parallel universe. The essence of playwriting is thinking theatrically, and creating plays by working in a theatrical way.

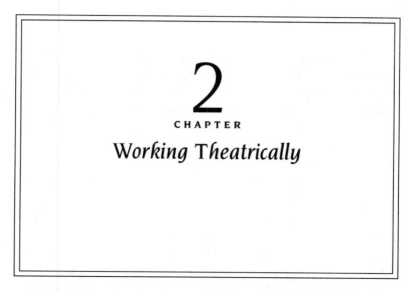

2

CHAPTER

Working Theatrically

LET'S MOVE NOW FROM THE CEREBRAL TOWARD THE APPLIED,
going from thinking theatrically to working theatrically. Such a move
requires some background on the concept of theatre games for
playwrights, which is at the heart of this book.

It has been my experience that the advice of many playwriting
books can be doctrinaire or even nontheatrical. Doctrinaire statements include saying, "the conflict must begin by page 5," or that
exposition has to be done in such and such a way. Nontheatrical
statements are suggesting that you develop plots from outlines or
work up characters from lists of traits such as hair color, politics,
and choice of bath soap.

I won't deny that a playwright can work from these kinds of
methodologies, but they don't work for me or most of the writers
and teachers I know around the country. I get lost in outlines or
want to deviate from them when working on the script itself. And
too often lists remain just lists. When I eventually became committed to playwriting, I searched for a way of exploring the world of
the play that was immediate and not abstract. This took me on a
fairly long process of discovery that I'll describe here in an abbre-
viated way.

I got started in theatre as a fledgling playwright who got talked
into playing a role in a community college production and fell
madly in love with performing. I spent several decades acting and
studying acting and directing.

I learned a great deal from a variety of theories and techniques in those years. Viola Spolin's theatre games and improvisations were the most consistently useful. Her theatre games showed me how to work from a "doing" approach—finding a given scene through active discovery—rather than a detached mental process. Improvisation taught me ways of redefining a scene and giving it a larger life as well. When a director had me improvise what happened after my character left a scene, for example, it opened my mind up to the larger life and possibilities in that scene and the entire play. My subsequent acting work benefited because the techniques helped me create a more informed, detailed, and theatrical world than I ever had before. When I learned how to develop a character through improvisation (such as setting up a "what if" situation or creating a prior circumstance), I found that my characterizations were far more textured. My characters were no longer defined merely by the words they said or the plot they existed in. They became more vital persons with more complete and larger lives and for whom the play was an extremely important period in that life, but only a portion of the whole.

Similarly, by directing with theatre games and improvs I discovered that there were any number of approaches to the problem of a given scene. If I saw my actors having difficulty getting at the feelings of a scene I could have them play a variety of theatre games. In this way I avoided a mechanical approach, or imposing my interpretation on their feelings. In essence, we solved a theatrical problem in a theatrical way.

In the late 1970s, I lucked into a situation that brought me back to playwriting. I was working as the stage manager at the Actors Studio, and one of the benefits was being able to observe (and eventually participate in) any workshops I wanted to there. This included the Directors Unit, which was then under the guidance of the legendary Harold Clurman, and the newly formed Playwrights Unit, which had been created by Israel Horovitz. Every Monday evening for a year, I watched this group of ten playwrights working together on new plays (Horovitz's concept was for everyone in the group to start a new play at the same time and work on ten pages per week). I often served as an actor for them.

I learned a great deal watching these writers develop their scripts, but as time went on I felt that something wasn't working. It seemed to me that the writers talked to each other too often in terms of how they would have written the other's play rather than dealing with the real theatrical problems of a given script.

Jeffrey Sweet, one of the writers, was experiencing similar feelings and was planning on trying a different approach to this kind of workshop. He invited me to join him. I admired Jeffrey's work very much, had acted in a play of his written in the Playwrights Unit, had directed a scene from yet another in the Directors Unit, and felt confident that he knew his way around. I accepted his invitation.

The workshop (which later acquired the wonderful title of the New York Writers' Bloc) was built around the same solid ten-pages-per-week concept of Mr. Horovitz but went a step further by including actors and directors as members. Consequently, the Bloc's critiques were more focused on craft questions and issues, having to do with an actor saying, for example, "I was able to pursue my objective in this scene very clearly until this line, where I contradict everything I'd said previously."

This gave the writer essential input that was not about trying to rewrite the playwright's work but came from an artist who might be responsible for trying to make something truthful in production. It was about working theatrically.

One of the most important developments in the Writers' Bloc was the creation and evolution of the six-line, which is the conceptual foundation for the exercises in this book.

After we had met for about a year, some of us nonwriters began to want to try some writing without having to go through the horrors of a critique. This was when the six-line was introduced. I believe it was Jeffrey Sweet who came up with this innovation. The six-line was based on a simple theatre game used for improvisations.

The six-line as a writing exercise is a short scene literally comprised of six lines between two characters—with each character having three lines. A line can be one word or five pages (though less is more, of course) and is the sum of one character's thoughts as spoken in that one response.

Each week's six-lines were based on a given topic, which was also known as a negotiation. A negotiation was defined as the matter, issue, or problem between two people who each wanted a different result and automatically led to conflict, which is the essence of dramatic writing. It also led to writing that was balanced because both characters had active stakes in the situation. In other words, each wanted something and no character was passive.

The use of an assigned negotiation helped us all because we didn't have to think of a topic on our own, and it allowed each of us to react to a given topic in our own unique way. Most importantly, it kept us focused on the "show, don't tell" axiom because the six-line was intended to actively engage characters in a problem-solving situation rather than just have them say words to each other.

A crucial concept underlying the negotiations is something I really want to stress here because it's the core concept of this book: the negotiation is what the characters use to talk through. What they may be saying in the text is "I never met an oyster I could love," while their subtext is "You know this is a food I detest, you ordered it for me anyway, and you did it in a public situation where I can't really holler at you!"

The negotiation is the center of all theatrical writing because it allows the audience to draw conclusions from what the characters say and do rather than just have them say it directly. Choose virtually any play you like and look at how the characters behave in their conflicts and you will see negotiations: "I want X and I'll do Y to get it" is pitted against "I won't let you have X unless you give me Z."

To make this clearer, I've written two six-lines based on board games as the negotiation. I've chosen this negotiation because it's naturally competitive and because the two variations attempt to show how different the subtextual competitions (above and beyond the games) can be. It may be a given that A wants to beat B and vice versa in whatever board game they're playing—that's the nature of a game—but it's not a given as to why or how each wants to win, and that's where the negotiation reveals the nature of the plot and character.

The following examples will give a clearer sense of how a negotiation works. They also show the essential format and ground rules, the most basic ground rules being to use a simple negotiation, to use two characters only, to give both characters strong objectives, to keep the length between six and ten lines, and to keep the scene active.

#1. *A couple playing Scrabble.*
KAREN: There. L-O-V-E. That's, mm, double letter, fifteen.
HARRY: OK, and I'll just borrow that L, and add my U, S, T. That's triple word, forty-five!
KAREN: Fine! I'll add my F, U, and L up here. That's now *Faithful*, and that scores me thirty-six, so I'm still up by fifty.
HARRY: Yeah? Well, here's one for you—in front of your ART, I drop a P, then finish with a Y. Double word, triple letter on the Y, and we're talking seventy-eight points. Now who's "up"?
KAREN: Yeah, we'll see. Here, try this: in front of your ANT I'm going to add P, R, E, G, N. [A beat; she gives him a very long look.] Your move. [Beat.] Well?
HARRY: I'm thinking! [Beat.] I'm thinking.

#2 *Two guys playing Monopoly.*
[Louis rolls the dice, counts off the squares, and throws his hands up in anguish.]
LOUIS: Park Place again! Jeez, I'm gonna be busted.
FRED: That . . . depends.
LOUIS: Depends? On what?
FRED: [Super casual.] Well, I mean, I'd hate to see this end your streak of—how many?
LOUIS: You know how many. [Beat.] All right, forty-nine! Forty-nine! [Beat.] All right, already! Depends on what?
[Fred makes a driving gesture.]
LOUIS (Cont.): Heyyyy, nobody drives The Wanderer but yours truly—
FRED: [Over him.] Just for one special night for Melissa, it's her birthday: your car or—bummer—the end of the streak . . .
[A pause, then Louis crumbles, holds out his keys; Fred smiles and takes them.]

Now, setting aside any debate over how great these exercises may or may not be, they do obey the basic rules of the six-line form while doing some other things as well. For instance, both of the six-lines reveal qualities about the characters without having the characters announce those qualities—we just see it in the way they each react to their side of the negotiation. We also see how the characters use language, how serious they are about their particular negotiation, and so on.

Most importantly, however, the six-lines exemplify the notion of working theatrically, which is what we're talking about in this chapter. A problem is set up: show a relationship through a board game. The solution is not a doctrine or a list but a theatrical process.

The consequent extensions of the six-line—the exercises in this book—evolved from observation of the working processes of various playwrights in the Writers' Bloc and elsewhere.

For example, I watched one playwright work on characters by writing a series of monologues for each one, just to hear how they spoke and felt about themselves. Another worked on exposition by writing the scene in which the prior event had occurred—even though this scene would never appear in the play—and it dawned on me finally that this was exactly like the kind of improvisations and theatre games I had done as an actor and director except these were written. Eureka! I had a whole other variety of negotiations to play with.

Why hadn't it occurred to me before the Writers' Bloc to use these techniques for writing? I think it was because, like most people, I was taught that you just had to write a certain way: you sit, you stare at the page, consult your outline, and then you write. Nobody had ever suggested that there were other approaches to the act of writing or even the act of thinking about writing. For me, the six-line and related exercises did something special by stressing the word "act" above any other; act, as in active.

This active process allows the writer to explore the play, the characters, events prior to or following the play, and so on—all in a very theatrical way because the exploration itself is through playwriting. It isn't sitting around making a list of who your main character would vote for but having the character argue for that vote in a monologue so that you can experience the creation of how that character talks and feels about the vote and reveals a sense of self through the talking. In the process of writing this monologue, you could find out what kind of vocabulary the character has, what the frame of reference is, what political viewpoint the person takes, and even who the character decided to argue this point with. You have the option of trying to capture the sound of someone you've met or to create a character from scratch but, regardless, you are doing it theatrically. This monologue might or might not be part of the play you intend to write, but you will know this character more as a living person for your play because you have endowed that character with an active, dramatic life: a list is only a list, but a character speaking is a human being experienced immediately, directly, and theatrically.

Before ending this chapter, I would be remiss if I didn't acknowledge once again that theatre games are only one way of working. Some playwrights work quite successfully with outlines or by putting scenes and even beats on notecards. It is crucial that you discover for yourself what will work for you. In this same spirit, I would suggest that you read a variety of other books on playwriting. Though some may strike you as rigid in their methodologies, all of them will have something you can learn from, if only on the most basic level.

This book puts the control of the choices of technique in the hands of the playwright rather than in the doctrine of a given author or teacher, including your humble narrator. I find that very exciting because it gives the playwright so much more latitude and artistic muscle. It offers a wide variety of possible explorations, which can be used in a multitude of ways, and it keeps the focus consistently on process. And there simply is no art without control of process on the part of the artist.

Ask artists who have practiced their craft for more than a few years and they will tell you that inspiration has a nasty habit of disappearing. With a thorough mastery of your own process, however, the creative effort can be sustained at a high level at all times and inspiration will feel more inclined to stick around. Further, the exercises are ways of working on one's play beyond the initial discovery process—they are helpful explorations for rewriting, which is always a tricky area for any writer.

It needs to be said that while this concept of working through exercises evolved out of workshop experiences, it is not absolutely tied to workshopping. I think workshops can be the best of all possible worlds for playwrights, but they are often highly subjective worlds. I would advise people going into a workshop environment to have a strong sense of their own techniques, needs, and ego before making any leaps. You'll find a more thorough discussion of workshops in Chapter 8. Suffice it to say for now that the best of what workshops can provide is a consistency of truth in craft.

The exercises in this book form a basis for testing your truth in craft and enhancing it. Even more, they provide a way of expanding your perspective. It is axiomatic that writers work in solitude, and in such isolation it is easy to start taking shortcuts, or grow complacent. Working through the exercises provides a way of resisting such temptations.

Finally, the use of exercises is also a way to keep on working. Writers often experience dry patches (even writer's block, which is dealt with in Chapter 9). These exercises are a way of continuing to develop writing muscles even when there's no immediate project or idea on the horizon. Art is often about how you grow beyond the last project. Through using the exercises to challenge yourself, and trying to open up new channels, most playwrights should be able to avoid stagnation and repetition.

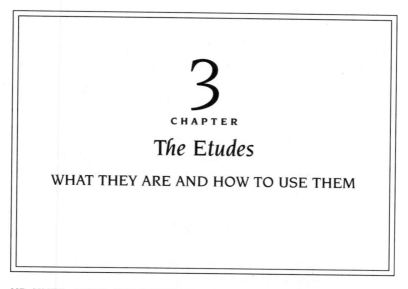

3

CHAPTER

The Etudes

WHAT THEY ARE AND HOW TO USE THEM

UP UNTIL NOW, I'VE REFERRED TO THE PROCESS THIS BOOK advocates as theatre games or exercises. Now I want to replace those terms with one that contains more important resonances for the playwright's craft: *etudes*.

The first logical step in learning any craft is to become familiar with the tools you'll be using. Etudes are the tools of theatre games, so here we're going to define and clarify a bit further the work process they're used for. The chapters that follow are compilations of etudes grouped by functions such as technique, plot, structure, and character.

What's an etude? For a musician, it's an exercise, such as scales, designed to strengthen key skills and techniques. In this sense, an etude is used more for sheer technical development than it is for the more subtle interpretive aspect of a player's skills. In other words, etudes for a given pianist won't make him better able to play the feeling of the "Moonlight Sonata," but they should make him better able to play the notes precisely and with the requisite dexterity. The etudes in this book apply to playwriting by refining technique—what a jazz musician might call "developing your chops."

For a painter, an etude may be used as preparation for a larger work rather than a basic skill-building exercise; it is, literally, a study. Georges Seurat was one painter who worked this way; he prepared dozens of etudes for his masterworks, such as the famous *Sunday Afternoon on the Island of La Grande Jatte*. In order to have a fuller sense of the elements of this huge work, Seurat did a series of much smaller paintings that explored qualities such as shape, color, tonality, and balance. The painterly use of etudes applies already developed essential skills in order to attempt an untried new vision or level of endeavor.

Another use for etudes is sensory exploration. Actors are routinely trained in sensory work to give them access to a range of choices in their personal memories or in their imaginations through the senses of sight, hearing, taste, smell, and touch. Writers also do this kind of sensory work intuitively because they tend to draw on their own experiences for their writing, but this work often lacks refinement because it's not done consciously. Many of the etudes in this book are for the purpose of provoking conscious sensory exploration.

Etudes help build techniques necessary for a greater range of expression and provide a way of experimenting with new applications of your expression. How a given etude can help depends on the ultimate demands and complexity of the piece being attempted. As importantly, it will depend on how well the artist utilizes and extends the potential of the chosen etudes. But how does a playwright use etudes?

In Chapter 2 I suggested writing a monologue for a character who talks about how he would vote in an election. As the writer, I could approach this exercise in a number of ways based on what kind of sensory work I want to do for myself and for my character. One choice would be simply to write a monologue that tries to express the views of the character. Other possibilities include:

- Setting up an environment, improvising the monologue on the spot, and recording it for memory's sake.

- Writing a scene in which two people are arguing over who to vote for.

- Writing different scenes in which your main character is twenty-one, then fifty, then seventy-five to explore the changes in that character's political point of view.

- Writing a scene for the character in two different situations: in the first, the character would be simply a voter, and in the second the character would be a voter who has also been a campaign worker for the chosen candidate. You could complicate this latter situation by writing pre-election, post-defeat or post-victory variations.

- Writing a monologue or scene of your own memories of voting for the first time or of working for a candidate.

- Writing a monologue or scene based on a character voting for the first time in a country in which elections had been banned.

These are just some of the potential choices. Each has its possibilities, and some are clearly more dramatic and stimulating than others.

Regardless, all of the choices are kinds of improvisations or sensory work. Each asks you to find the truth of a character's experiences by getting into his mind and feelings, and each asks you to place your character in a real dramatic world in which he has a stake or a problem to solve. Each asks you to be the character and see the world actively from that point of view, which effectively puts you in that world. This is clearly not the same as writing a list of who the character would vote for or even a prose narrative of some kind about the character. Instead, you are challenged to put on the character's shoes and walk around in them: you have the theatrical equivalent of a direct experience.

It's important to keep one idea in sight through all of this: etudes are for exploration. You'll need to remember that none of these monologues or scenes might ever appear in your play. There's no rule that says you can't use them, but the primary purpose of etudes is for groundwork. You don't need to worry about whether a given etude "works" as a product because the true measure is how the etude works as a process. We talk in theatre quite frequently in terms of performance being the tip of the iceberg. It means we assume that a good actor will have done perhaps ten times the work necessary to create the role than is needed to actually perform the role. The actor who has approached the role through such a thorough process will create a character who is more complete and deeply textured than will the actor who merely rehearses the play. In the same manner, the etudes help you dig into your creation in a thorough and theatrical way so that you have crafted a textured, layered, and truthful work.

Using the etudes is a matter of individual choice. One simple application is as a practice for the basic skills of playwriting, like finger exercises for a pianist. A complete novice could do all of the etudes in this book and come away from the experience with a much richer idea of the techniques of playwriting because the etudes challenge you to solve basic problems. A seasoned playwright might do the etudes and rediscover forgotten techniques or even find new ones that could lead to a reexploration of style, content, or work process. Any veteran playwright will tell you that each play means a reinvestment in the basics while struggling to find new ways of using those basics to evolve new levels of expression. The etudes can provide this by challenging routine ways of thinking.

Another application is for the writer who is blocked. There is a chapter of etudes aimed directly at the blocked writer, but etudes in the other chapters could also be very helpful because the emphasis of the etudes is on process and exploration, and not product.

The etudes can also be helpful as a simple way of discovering ideas for stories. You could do an assortment of etudes for fun, and discover a connection that might lead to an idea or two. It's not a guaranteed thing of course, but I have often found that ideas can present themselves if I just write, even if my mind seems unfocused at the time. Our subconscious reveals itself to us through art. By practicing a process or discipline such as these etudes, our other layers become known to us as well. There is a chapter dedicated to plot etudes but story ideas may come from any of these exercises. Similarly, there is a chapter for character etudes, but who's to say exactly what will trigger a character into life for you?

How do you work with the etudes in the chapters that follow? My first suggestion would be to just read through them, perhaps even at random. Try picking out pages blindfolded, for instance. I can't stress enough that the basis for all of this is playing at writing. Viola Spolin created theatre games because the fundamental concept of theatre itself is a game: it has rules, true, but within those parameters the essence is fun.

Whether you read the etudes willy-nilly or in sequence, try an etude when you hit one that tickles your fancy. Then try some of the referenced and linked etudes which are related to that one and see where they take you. These meanderings will automatically take you into various places in the book and get you into the concept of the etudes a little further.

From there, you can go in a hundred directions. You could continue doing etudes for the sheer fun of it or begin to use them in a more dedicated and systematic way by looking for etudes to help you explore a problem in a play you're working on or planning to work on.

One very strenuous suggestion must be made here: practice a system of doing the etudes first and analyzing the results afterwards. Analysis is extremely useful in this way of working, but it will only impede your process if you start trying to out-think the etude before trying it. Once you have a grasp of the basic idea of the etude, commit yourself to trying it without advance planning. Afterwards, you may realize you've discovered a variety of things you hadn't previously considered, which would be ideal. But the main goal is to come to the etudes with an open mind.

The etudes are grouped into units. If you are currently working on a play, you may already have a very clear idea of your plot but feel your characters need fleshing out. This would be the obvious time to try a variety of character etudes. The converse would be true if you have a character who intrigues you but who lacks a plot to set him in motion.

Then again, you may have everything in place except how to start the play, and there you sit facing the accursed blank screen or page. You might find an etude, any etude, and use it to start your play—even choosing one entirely at random can give your characters a reason to start interacting. I frequently start plays with a simple six-line just to get going, often using the first negotiation that pops into my head. It's true that I often end up cutting that first beat in a subsequent rewrite, but the point is I stopped sitting there worrying and got down to actual writing.

And that may be the last philosophical point to make here: writers make themselves crazy wanting to write it perfectly the first time.

Well, forget it. Some plays do write themselves, but most of them take a long time and many drafts to finally say something coherent—that's just the nature of the beast. Etudes have often come to my rescue because they naturally lead to a deepening of process in a clear, focused way. In other words, you're already lost in this play, so why not get lost creatively?

An ideal extension of this concept would be to come up with your own etudes to work from and to synthesize some of mine and some of yours. I still use a number of Spolin's exercises when I direct, but I add variations as well to serve the needs of the particular play and company. The point is to do what works, throw out what doesn't, and make up the rest as you go along. Hey, it's art, not accounting. That's the joy of it.

It's been my experience that each play I've written has been a combination of old ground and new turf. The etudes can help with the new turf because their nature is exploratory, but I believe the etudes can be solid foundations for the old ground as well. Every time we write a play, the same basic craft concepts have to be applied, and we need to remember those concepts over and over again. The etudes are rooted firmly in such craft concepts as "show, don't tell," "less is more," "jump into the action late," and so on, and thus are a good way of reinforcing these concepts in an organic way.

This is why it's crucial to eventually read through all the etudes, and try as many as you can. Until you really spend time learning how to use the power drill or the socket wrench, they're of little value to you when you're actually working on a project. Once you know what to use and when, there's no hesitation. What you choose truly will be a useful tool.

Finally, remember that the etudes will not automatically give you better plays, although I contend they should be better because you'll be more in control of your techniques. You will also not get any kind of quick fix—you may have to search for a while before any given etude helps you with a specific problem, if at all. What you will get is more control, muscle, ability, and dexterity as a playwright—a crafter of plays—and more range as a theatrical thinker and worker.

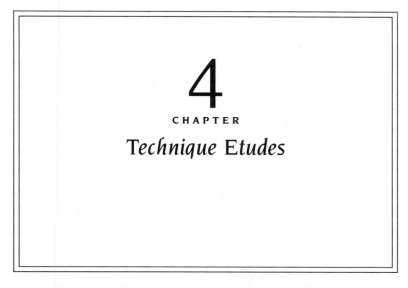

4

CHAPTER

Technique Etudes

THE ETUDES IN THIS CHAPTER ARE AIMED AT DEVELOPING A range of basic skills and techniques for playwriting. They are also useful exercises for thinking about a play or its characters before writing the script and for continuing to explore the plot or characters once you're into the script.

The main purpose of these technique exercises is to start you thinking theatrically, which is why I've put them first. Thinking theatrically is not just for the novice, however. All playwrights need to return to the basics over and over, so these are etudes that everyone can keep for craft maintenance as well. No matter how or when you use this initial set of etudes, you will find that their focus is generally more on the process of writing—what I call technique—than on writing toward a particular project. However, I hasten to add that it's not inconceivable that these etudes could lead you to the discovery of a plot or a character for a play. Take inspiration where you find it.

My primary advice for this chapter and the other etude chapters is to read through the whole chapter first to get a sense of what's in it and to see which etudes grab your imagination right off the bat. More than anything else, I want this book to be a stimulator and a catalyst. Perhaps that will happen for you on an intuitive basis first and then on a more planned basis as you grow more familiar with the etudes. Perhaps you need more structure from the start. Regardless, a given etude really has to leap out at you if it's going to be of any value to your needs and process, and this will probably happen only when you've had a chance to examine the scope of a given chapter.

As for the actual use of the etudes, I have a variety of suggestions. If you are a neophyte, I would suggest doing all of these etudes in any order that appeals to you. They should lead you to discover some essential ideas and skills necessary to playwriting. Each exercise has been written out in detail as to how to do the basic etude, what area you might be exploring, and what the potential results might be from its process. However, you may find that they lead to applications I don't cover, or questions I don't answer, which is when the etudes will begin to belong to you.

I'll also provide suggestions as to whether the etude is likely to be better for new work, for something previously written, or for both. I propose variations on the primary etude to help you extend the exercise and yourself. And I include a cross reference section at the end to guide you toward etudes I think are related to this one.

It is crucial that you not worry about getting an etude "right." Keep in mind that it's not results but the exploration and the process that matter. Each etude should provide you with an aspect of the various skills needed as a playwright. This is the key: it's up to you to make the connections and to determine how a given etude can serve your particular needs. What's right for you might not work for anyone else. I have my own ideas about how these should be applied, of course—some of which will be more than obvious by what categories I've placed certain etudes in—but I've tried to refrain from forcing the result of any etude.

To help you focus your exploration, I begin each chapter with a "key etude"—one basic etude by which to understand the rest in that chapter and to stress the process and exploration I have in mind.

For example, the key etude in this chapter is called Stage Directions Only and is primarily aimed at developing a crucial technique for a playwright: becoming more adept at using character actions and behavior rather than dialogue for telling a story. It is a way of getting you to think about story-telling without relying strictly on dialogue and suggests that your writing should combine dialogue and behavior for a more powerful use of the stage. It further suggests that in an instance where your impulse is to tell something in your script, you should try to show it instead, making your audience into active watchers rather than passive listeners.

What if you find applications for Stage Directions Only other than the ones I've outlined above? That's wonderful. I'm just providing a kind of rumpus room here. Again, what you do with it and what you want to get out of it are entirely up to you.

More experienced playwrights might also consider trying all of these etudes in a random fashion but from a somewhat different perspective than the tadpoles: try doing them with a view toward discovering which of your skills are in need of sharpening or rethinking. My personal experience with writing workshops and classes has been that they have two equally important functions: one is to discuss what works and doesn't work with a given play and the other is to serve as a reminder of craft basics. Whether you are in a workshop or not, these etudes can provide those very same kinds of reminders about craft essentials.

In addition, I think the etudes challenge habit. We all have our ways of working. Some are useful, but others may be getting in the way of working with real creative freedom. These etudes can be used to discover old habits and generate new ones. For instance, do you use behavior well and in place of (or in combination with) dialogue? Is your dialogue dramatic language or just talk? Do you really explore your characters? Is your tendency to write a single-plot play, or do you texturize your work by layering subplots?

I know each person will find individual applications for these exercises. Don't be afraid to experiment. Don't be afraid of your impulses. Above all, don't be afraid to have fun. Leap in and analyze later.

Finally, remember that after the key etude the etude sequence is alphabetical. This avoids stressing any etude and makes finding a given etude easier when you return to a chapter.

KEY ETUDE
Stage Directions Only

This etude presents an original exploration of a situation or rewrites an existing scene. As a rewrite, the purpose is to figure out how to minimize or eliminate dialogue while concentrating on behavior.

The Etude

Write or rewrite a scene in which the characters do not speak but convey their thoughts through behavior. For example, a scene with a couple having a fight could be done nonverbally if he's constantly working the TV remote in a hostile way while she's doing everything possible to disturb the TV reception and his concentration. Your primary job is to explore the mannerisms of your characters through their physical expression while telling a story without words.

The focus of the etude is to write stage directions that describe both activity and behavior. I define "activity" as simply doing: "She opens an envelope." This is just a necessary action to get to read the letter inside. Behavior is doing with subtext: "She rips open the envelope anxiously," or "He slowly tears the envelope to pieces without opening it." Behavior is activity endowed with meaning based on the internal process of the character: when characters show what they are thinking. Of course, "behavior" has nothing to do with misbehaving—being "bad"—or behaving—being "good." Certainly there can be behavior full of malice or angelic intent, but the primary issue is focusing on the way in which a person reveals thought and subtext through a given physical activity.

Behavior can also endow the object(s) in the activity with meaning, to make the object, in effect, another character or an extension of the character using it. A sword used by one character to hurt another represents that menacing character even when left on stage by itself because it has been endowed with that meaning. Without the endowment, it may suggest the meaning but not as clearly: a sword may be just a harmless ornament. With endowment, anything can take on additional meaning, so a feather duster that has been used as a weapon becomes as potent and menacing as any sword.

The point is to remember that the whole stage must be charged with meaning and purpose—and there is far more power in the ability of behavior to convey this meaning and purpose than there is in the ability of dialogue alone to do so.

This etude makes it necessary for the writer to focus strictly on the stage and its use by the characters rather than on talk. The stage directions must have the characters doing something that progresses and that reveals the mental state or intention of the characters. For example, a character who is cleaning all of his belongings, including wiping each page of his books, shows an obsessive nature. If we see at some point something that suggests the character has done away with someone, then the behavior becomes even more motivated because the purpose of the obsession becomes clearer.

Note that it is crucial for this exercise that you not create situations in which actors following your directions would have to start doing pantomime to make things clear—like pointing to a wrist to ask what time it is. The issue is to explore how behavior can communicate in ways that words cannot and not just substitute actions for language. Free yourself from the need for dialogue. When you can show something onstage rather than describe or talk about it, the power of the stage becomes more potent simply because the audience is experiencing it directly.

Remember, you can do this as an original exploration or as a rewrite of an existing piece. A rewrite of something already in dialogue form will allow you to reexplore the scene from a completely new perspective: what is this scene about in a strictly behavioral sense? Once you've done this exploration, you can then integrate your discoveries back into the scene and make a stronger marriage of your original dialogue with the behavior you've discovered. You may even find you want to eliminate much of the dialogue. Conversely, you might find you don't wish to integrate this newly discovered behavior or change a single word of your original scene—all of the etudes are designed for exploration and finding a new perspective; implementation of what evolves from your work is entirely up to you.

If you're doing the exercise for original material rather than for a rewrite, you have the option of trying to tell a complete story with a beginning, middle, and end or of isolating one event without concerning yourself with structure. Either way, the etude can be very helpful for exposing the personalities of your characters, for providing you with an awareness of what things (furniture and props) need to be in the environment to assist and enhance the behavior, and for discovering where you do or don't need dialogue.

Remember that although this etude may suggest slapstick comedy, that isn't the only avenue. A deadly serious, totally silent behavioral scene could be devastatingly grim or scary. A thorough exploration would show you the range of possibilities; don't go for the obvious or easy choices.

SEE ALSO: Adaptation Etudes; Behavior to Inevitable Words; Entrances and Exits; Place Explorations; Prop Etude; Secret Behavior.

OTHER ETUDES
Adaptation Etude 1: Prose Treatment
The main concept behind these adaptation etudes is to flip what's normal for you on its head by changing the primary mode of expression for your material. This etude is for plays that are simply not working. With this etude you have a technique to try to find your way back to your original impulse and ideas when you've gotten lost.

The Etude
If your draft just feels wrong, try writing the play out as a treatment. By trying to capture the idea of the play in a prose form, you may be able to spot the problems with your piece.

Let me say immediately that a treatment is not a short story. It's a prose version of a dramatic work, which means that it tells the story without a lot of descriptive, adjective-laden language. The point of a treatment is to get the nuts and bolts down: it reports the story from A to Z, gives a very succinct description of the characters, and provides a sense of the tone of the piece (i.e., impressionistic drama or screwball comedy). Most treatments are limited to two to three pages. You should limit yourself to this range because that kind of precision is an excellent discipline for a writer.

There's one other aspect you might find very helpful if you've lost the handle on your play: writing a treatment as a sales pitch. Try writing about your play as if you're trying to sell it to a producer or artistic director. What would make them the most excited about the play? What, in fact, makes you the most excited about the play? The point is to get yourself back to the original catalyst for writing the play. Something got you going and set your imagination firing—

what was it? Once you have a better sense of what that something was, it is often easier to relocate the play you originally intended.

Variations

Try the same approach verbally. Ask a friend to listen to you describe the play in detail so that both of you can listen for where you're focused and fired up and where you're confused, unenthused, or just all wet. However, this will still work best if you keep to the treatment disciplines of brevity and precision—make the form work for you.

Another approach is to write a treatment before starting a play, but I would only recommend this if you're not sure of your story or tone. As I've said before, some friends of mine use this technique with success but it doesn't work for me; you'll need to discover the potential on your own.

SEE ALSO: Adaptation Etudes, Adapting to the Stage Etudes.

Adaptation Etude 2: Radio Play

Radio Play is an etude primarily for use on a scene from a play that is not working, although it can be used to do original work.

This etude imposes very interesting limitations on the writer because radio is purely aural. The joy of Radio Play is seeing how clever you can be in finding ways of using sound to convey your story. The trap is having characters explain everything to a listener, and you must avoid this temptation. If you're not familiar with radio as a dramatic form, I'd recommend listening to recordings of old radio shows. The Orson Welles Mercury Theatre material shows a tremendous amount of adapting theatre to radio. I'd also suggest choosing dramas over comedies since the dramas had to rely more on sound than the comedies did. There is also excellent quality radio drama on National Public Radio; how much is offered varies from locale to locale, but there are recordings available.

Your first option is to do an adaptation of the piece you've been working on, and the second is to write an original piece just to play with the medium. Regardless, the pleasure of writing for radio is learning how to wed dialogue and sound to convey a story, much like learning to put behavior and dialogue together. The real challenge is to find as many ways to utilize sound primarily as you can. In other words, rather than having someone announce that it's breakfast time, what kinds of sounds would automatically convey that fact? In addition, sound is necessary to set mood—whether you set a mood of depression by using the lonely moan of a fog horn or a blues tune is up to you, but the key is allowing sound to do it and making innovative sound choices.

The Etude

Adapt a scene from an existing play into a radio play. This should be a scene that's giving you trouble, but it could just be a scene that you want to fool around with some more. Adhere strictly to the radio form: use a combination of sound and dialogue to tell your story and avoid having a narrator describe everything to us.

There are many potential results from this exercise. Through it you may discover the need for sound to help a scene that's not clear enough in terms of mood, or you may discover that the scene is too talky—just listening rather than watching and listening can be very instructive. Further, having to rethink it entirely into a different medium may provide you with new ways of looking at the scene. Lastly, I think radio is a medium with potential that remains to be fully explored, and maybe you'll find an interest in it as well through this etude.

Variations

Have some actor friends improvise your scene as a radio piece. Let them have the nuts and bolts of the scene, then turn them loose with sound effects materials to see what happens. In any case, you would probably benefit greatly from having your adaptation or their improvisation recorded and played back like a radio show. Sometimes depriving yourself of one or more sensory aspects of your work can open up all kinds of doors.

Do an original scene just for radio as a way of exploring the medium. This is a good way of developing some techniques that will pay off in later work and a solid method of rethinking the medium of the stage.

SEE ALSO: Adaptation Etudes, Behavior to Inevitable Words, Secret Behavior, and Stage Directions Only.

Adaptation Etude 3: Silent Movie

This is a direct application of the Stage Directions Only etude and a nice variation on the Radio Play exercise above. The etude assumes you have some understanding of and respect for silent film style. I'd strongly recommend studying the form if you're not familiar with it. Chaplin's comedies are excellent, as are the dramas by D. W. Griffith, C. B. DeMille, and Abel Gance, just to name a few. I would also caution you to keep the material you're adapting fairly short. There would be little purpose in adapting a full-length play.

The Etude

Adapt a scene from an original play into a silent movie. You can also write an original piece directly for silent movie form, which I'll talk more about below. Again, this can be a scene that is driving you crazy or that you just want to shake up a little. Regardless, putting a scene into this very disciplined form is going to show you a lot.

In this etude you are pursuing several goals. One goal is converting dialogue to visual communication to help you see how much of the dialogue from your original scene you really need. Dealing with the issue of adaptation is another goal. Adaptation is basically a reaction to a given work: if you decide to adapt someone's novel, for instance, the resultant piece will be your version of that novel. Silent Movie gets you to write a version of your own original scene. This will allow you to see what you think is essential and nonessential about that scene, in the same way that adapting a novel would cause you to jettison subplots that wouldn't work while you focus on piecing together a plotline that will. This adaptation process will give you a fresh look at the story you're trying to tell and purge stuff that may be getting in the way.

In addition, I sometimes feel that writers get too hung up on symbols and layers of meaning while sacrificing or obscuring the main story. (I'm not antisymbol or even antiobscurity; I'm just interested in the nature of artistic choices.) Adaptation necessitates a laser focus on the story because it's the thing you're trying to carry from one form to another—and this may help you reveal a story that has gone a bit astray. Conversely, if your interest is purely in symbolism, Silent Movie will be useful because it will allow you to test out other ways of looking at your symbols from the broad perspective of the stage to the far more limited focus of the camera lens to see if they continue to work or not. Many early silent films like *The Cabinet of Dr. Caligari* or M were highly symbolic, so there are precedents on which to draw.

The game plan is to rewrite your original piece using silent film techniques. You can occasionally include captions (but only occasionally) so that an audience seeing the film with or without them would understand the same essential dramatic points. By virtue of the medium, your focus must be predominantly on the visual, and so the discipline of doing this etude is in moving your story from a full sensory to a limited sensory form.

The point is to get a fresh perspective on a given piece. You may have a scene that feels talky and lifeless, and this etude is a great method of finding ways to make the scene more alive. For example, if your scene involves two people simply sitting and talking for ten minutes, you probably don't have something that will go easily into a silent film style. Or do you? First of all, what are they talking about? Is it mostly exposition? If so, then make the adaptation about showing the actual events of the exposition by using flashbacks. Are they talking because they're plotting to hold up a bank? Then make the plot active in the adaptation: show them casing the joint, looking at plans, and practicing opening safes. Are they sitting around talking about what "it" all means? Then you probably have a problem, because this kind of scene won't adapt to a silent film style well. However, that alone might be quite telling: your scene may be simply undramatic and only talky. In which case it may be time to go back to the drawing board and rethink the whole deal. Do we need the scene, does it move the play forward, is it engaging for the audience, or does it just please you because the talk is so clever?

The adaptation aspect of this etude may yield a variety of results. Using the new information or new approach discovered from the silent film style to reshape or reinform the original scene is just one possibility for you to consider. Conversely, the discipline of the silent film form alone might be its own process and end. Regardless, whether you apply the etude back into the original or not, the process should open your thinking about structure, time frame, the use of images, the amount of dialogue, and so on. It's a great way of dragging your mind out of that deadly morass of Making-This-Damn-Play-Work and freeing up possibilities to let it work.

Variations

Take a relatively serious scene that you're having some trouble with and adapt it as a knock-around silent film comedy to loosen yourself up. It may be that your problem is being too heavy in the scene or not heavy enough—maybe inverting it will reveal the problem. Again, maybe it'll just free your mind from being too rigid about how the scene has to go.

You could also write something original for a silent movie as a stretching exercise. What's important and useful about this variation is that your intuitive choice of subject and situation will probably be quite right for a silent film. How could you adapt this piece for the stage? Can you make this etude go in the opposite direction? (See the Adapting to the Stage etudes in Chapter 6 for more on this.) Can you build your short silent piece into something bigger? Is there a movie inside that you didn't know about?

Regardless of how you use this etude, the issue will be to work in a different medium in order to rethink your original medium. Film thought is very different from theatrical thought, although they have many things in common. Exploiting one to reconsider the other should reveal many intriguing possibilities about both.

SEE ALSO: Adaptation Etudes, Adapting to the Stage Etudes, Behavior to Inevitable Words, Film Game, Film Reversal, Secret Behavior, and Stage Directions Only.

Behavior to Inevitable Words

This etude has a more directed focus than Stage Directions Only because it has a built-in point. In this etude your characters are avoiding talking because of a given situation and so the behavior itself is the avoidance. Or perhaps they cannot find means of saying what they're thinking so the behavior becomes the water-treading needed until those thoughts can be expressed. Regardless, when the characters can't stand the avoidance any longer or have come to where they can finally articulate their thoughts, they have reached a point where they must talk and that's the end of the etude (though it may not be the end of the scene, per se).

This etude is a very exciting way of putting your audience into the minds of the characters and is a good exploration into behavior. Where Stage Directions Only tells a story, this etude focuses more on a single event that may be the crest of a story that has been building: Liz is so mad at Ira that she's afraid to talk to him for fear she'll start screaming, so she takes it out on the housework while he tries to help her with it. The end result of this may be Ira realizing he's been a jerk and apologizing (so the etude would end with "I'm sorry"), or it may stop when Liz can finally say what's on her mind. Remember that the etude is based on letting the characters follow through on their behavior until—and only until—they must say something. It begins in midproblem and culminates with the dialogue when a major new beat begins. Whether that new beat would continue the problem or end it is irrelevant. Your goal is an exploration of the behavior to the fullest until one of the characters must finally speak.

The Etude

Write an original piece or rewrite an existing scene in which the characters are engaged in behavior based on avoiding words in some way. This behavior should lead inevitably to the words that are being avoided: "I'm sorry," "Get out!" or "I love you."

Your objective should be to find behavior that reveals the mental process of the characters. In other words, don't just have them do random activities until they finally talk. Try to find behavior that progresses toward the inevitable words. This is obviously a fun exploration of an argument-in-progress but it has other possible scenarios. Suppose, for instance, the issue is the inability to express feelings, such as saying "I love you," or "I'm scared." A man trying to find the courage to tell a woman he loves her might try to hint at it behaviorally in a variety of ways until he has to say it (this can even become comic if the woman is determined that he will say it.) The enjoyment for the audience, then, is waiting to see how it will turn out. The fun for you might be seeing how many ways you can make the guy in the scene screw up.

A vital aspect of this exercise is the actors' dictum that "You cannot play a negative." If I ask an actor what she's doing in a given scene, she might tell me "Oh, I'm not listening to her." To which my reply is "OK, so then what are you really doing?" It's impossible for a human being to perform a negative action. If someone says not to think about ice cream, your first impulse has to be to think about ice cream. Your second impulse will be to think of something instead of ice cream—a salad, say, if you're dieting. In other words, we cannot not listen. We can listen to something other than a given person or source, we can stop up our ears to block out the sound or we can make noises of our own to prevent the sound of the other person from getting in, but in every case, we are doing something that substitutes for what we don't want to hear.

The connection between not playing a negative and this exercise is in the avoidance aspect of the etude. Not every application of this etude has to be avoidance of course, but when it is, you're providing your characters with something to do that allows them to express the avoidance. "Instead of talking to you, I will get very busy cleaning house; now that you are insisting on talking to me, I will get totally obsessed with cleaning house." Avoidance is one of the most common human tendencies, and this etude lets you explore many possibilities for exploiting that tendency in a positive, active way.

It makes no difference whether you try this etude as an original exploration or as a way of reapproaching an existing scene—the discoveries should be of about the same quality. As an original exercise, you may discover some characters who are really fun to play with and who might be good for a play.

SEE ALSO: Adaptation Etudes, Comings and Goings, Entrances and Exits, Secret Behavior, and Stage Directions Only.

Composing to Music

This is one of my favorite etudes and very popular with my writing classes. This exercise works best when you let someone else choose the music, but it can be done on your own.

The Etude

Choose four different pieces of music (pieces that really clash in style and rhythm) and play each for a designated time period (e.g., five minutes), changing from one to the other with no pause. The writer's job is to start a scene and let it change according to the random influence of the music. This change could include having the characters talk about the music being played, but there are better uses of the etude. I try to discourage such an approach in classes.

The main purpose is to force you to work on a given scene with a set of variations that are externally imposed. In my class I use music choices that are in strong contrast to one another and which are themselves a bit jarring. My selections recently have been Pergolesi's "Stabat Mater," a celestial classical piece; Hüsker Dü's "Recurring Nightmare," a feedback-ridden and aptly named tune; "Mustt Mustt" by Nusrat Fateh Ali Khan, a mesmerizing version of Qawwali (Sufi) music; and "A Love Supreme" by John Coltrane, a jazz classic with sections that vary from rhythmically driving to just plain screaming and raw. None of these pieces has recognizable lyrics (except the chant "A love supreme" in the Coltrane piece) because I don't want lyrics to affect the writer's thought process or intrude on their words. This exercise frees the writer and takes students to places they wouldn't have gone on their own.

It's possible to do this exercise solo, but the element of surprise is pretty crucial. If you don't have a group situation available, try to have another person make a tape for you and avoid listening to it until trying the exercise.

Variations

With a radio, flip to different stations and go with the next tune you come to no matter what. Buy recorded music by somebody whose work you don't know and write to a sequence of cuts on the recording. Instrumental music or vocal pieces not in your own language are best.

SEE ALSO: Writing Lyrics.

Emotional Reversal

The concept for these etudes came from exercises used by the late Lehman Engel, who ran the BMI (Broadcast Music, Inc.) Musical Theatre Workshops for years. Mr. Engel was the American (if not the world) authority on musical theatre; his book *The Making of a Musical* (Macmillan Publishing Company, Inc., New York) is still a crucial work for anyone studying the form. Variations of this exercise were assigned regularly in his workshops.

What is particularly interesting here is the notion of playing against expectations, of using a surface to unveil a subsurface. Too often our writing exists on a flat plane and we ignore the variety of textures that we have available to play with. The Emotional Reversal etudes open up the possibilities of these textures.

The essence of the exercise is found in the first variation: create a comic scene that reveals a sad layer beneath the fun. A perfect example of this is in John Guare's *House of Blue Leaves*, in which the entire play functions as an emotional reversal. The increasingly manic and complicated life of Artie Shaughnessy is progressively funny to us until the last moment of the play hits us like a lightning bolt. In an unexpected moment the truths that have been lurking beneath the humor are shatteringly revealed.

It's not necessary for this emotional reversal to be the essence of an entire play; using it just for a scene or even a beat in a scene can be extremely effective as a way of revealing character and situation. Nor does emotional reversal imply a beat, scene, or play that must end with a revelation—that just happens to be the situation with Guare's play. The emotional reversal could be letting the bragging of a man reveal his insecurity or letting the extremely polite conversation of a couple reveal their deep animosity toward each other. In other words, the emotional reversal lets the audience see another level and does not rely on last-minute insights or twists per se.

The Etude

Emotional Reversal 1: Write a scene in which the context of the situation is comic but the resultant understanding (or feeling) of the situation is sad or serious. For example, consider a scene in which a troubled couple is laughingly sharing memories of an accident-ridden honeymoon. While the scene is funny, what gets revealed is that the honeymoon was a disaster and that the sharing of the memories now is painful and perhaps even emblematic of this marriage's disarray.

Emotional Reversal 2: write a scene in which the context of the situation is sad or serious but the resultant understanding (or feeling) of the situation is comic. The best example of this I know comes, oddly enough, from TV. In one *Mary Tyler Moore Show* episode, Chuckles the Clown dies while dressed as Mr. Peanut. Chuckles was "shelled" by an elephant, which triggers endless jokes.

Variations

Write a scene in which the context is angry but reveals tenderness or in which the text is polite but reveals a subtext of hatred, anger, or cynicism. Clearly, you can take this in as many directions as you can think of. But the heart of your effort must always be to deepen the texture of the scene you're creating.

This etude may also be used as a way of reattacking a scene you've already written but that doesn't work yet. If your feeling is that the scene is simply too straight to the point, an emotional reversal is a way of pulling the scene out of the linear and literal and making it more varied and dramatically suggestive. Regardless of how you use it, this etude will challenge you to put your work on a more complex level, which is always for the best.

SEE ALSO: Emotional Winds, Extreme Mood, Personal Problem, Personal Quality, Problem-Solving Monologue, Secret Behavior, Secret Past, Status Etude, and Word Choice.

Environmental Etude

This etude delves into the impact of environment on a given scene and set of characters. It may be done as an original piece or a rewrite.

The stress in this etude is on condition rather than locale, which is the subject of other etudes. There will be some overlap, naturally, since the two often go together—rainy weather and Seattle or intense dry heat and El Paso—but it's your job to emphasize the environment rather than the place. Environment breaks down into these two categories: climatic conditions, such as the temperature or weather, and circumstantial conditions, such as intense pollution, or a flood, or earthquake.

The Etude

Place some characters you want to explore or reexplore in an environmental extreme. Be sure to make the conditions something the characters cannot easily control, so that part of the objective becomes coping with those conditions. This limit will give you the opportunity to expose more about the nature of your characters and evolve possible situations for them.

If you're doing this etude with an existing scene or existing characters, the exercise should help you see if your original choices are as strong as they could be. You may, for instance, have your original play set during an "average" day. Would the play become stronger if the environment had a direct impact on the world of the play? In other words, would *Bus Stop* work without the blizzard? What if your play now takes place on the hottest day of the year or during a gigantic chemical spill? These thoughts may have no application, of course, but they are worth giving some consideration.

You could also work an interesting character through a variety of environments to see where she is content, cranky, or capable of coping. Perhaps your character is utterly stoic until faced with an infestation of cuckoos, or perhaps your character only feels alive when it's pouring down rain. All kinds of surprises may be out there. In any event, environment has a continual impact so it's a very useful exploration just to remind ourselves that neither we nor our characters live in hermetic vacuums.

SEE ALSO: Being There Etudes, Change of Time, Disaster, Emotional Winds, Extreme Mood, Place Explorations, Sensory Etudes, Situation Exploration, and Where Do I Live?

Familiarity Etude
This etude uses degrees of familiarity between the speakers as a basis. I will limit you to three levels of familiarity: high, middle, and low.

In high familiarity dialogue, the characters know each other extremely well—a married couple, say—and so will speak in a commonly understood language that requires little explanation: "Where's the thing?" "By the coffee." "He called?" "Right after you." This exchange would be understood by the characters in high familiarity to mean that the insurance information brochure (the thing) is in the kitchen on the counter by the coffee pot, and that the insurance agent called this morning at about 10:15, immediately after the two characters had spoken by phone. Conversely, in low familiarity dialogue, the characters don't know each other at all, so they will tend to speak in a language that is searching for common ground and many things must be explained until commonly understood. Lastly, middle-familiarity dialogue occurs between people who only know each other on a limited basis: co-workers who don't socialize with each other, for instance. They may only share a common language related to their work experiences.

What's the point of this etude? Knowing what familiarity level your characters are in helps you discover the nature of the language they'll speak in a given scene. Further, if you have exposition you need to get across to your audience, it will be of greater use to introduce a low- or middle-familiarity scene than a high-familiarity one at that point, simply because in high-familiarity mode information is less likely to be exchanged. In other words, you don't tell your significant other things like "Your name is Ellen, you've been married to me for nine years, and we have two kids named Spike and Sadie." If it's ludicrous to do this in life, it's even more so in theatre. And yet we see examples all the time.

The degree of familiarity also gives the audience information on how to watch something. If we know the truth about an event and see one person lie about it to her spouse, what had been high familiarity gets flip-flopped into low familiarity: she didn't tell him the truth; she knows something he doesn't. Now we want to know why she's lying and so we become directly involved in the shift of familiarity ourselves. Further, familiarity gives us varying points of view. How a character presents himself to other people in high-, low-, and middle-familiarity shows us much about him—great variation shows us that he's not real somehow, while great continuity shows us a person of seemingly steadfast qualities.

Exploring the potential in each level of familiarity will give you a much stronger grip on how to use that familiarity. One exploration you can do is read plays with familiarity as your main focus, and I'd suggest two choices for starters. *Betrayal* by Harold Pinter is an extraordinary exercise in varying familiarities; in fact, it might be argued that the strain between actual familiarities and assumed familiarities is a great part of what dictated the structure of the play. Marsha Norman's '*Night, Mother* studies how people can live cheek-by-jowl in seemingly high familiarity and yet know nothing of each other.

The Etude

Create an event (such as a car accident on a suburban street) that people would observe and then talk about. Your job will be to create three different relationships, one at each specific familiarity level. Then write a dramatic scene in which the members of each relationship discuss their observations of the event. Relationship 1 is high-familiarity and might have a couple using the accident as an excuse to continue their endless argument over who drives worse. Relationship 2 is low-familiarity. You might have two strangers argue about the sequence of the events of the accident or other details. Relationship 3 is middle-familiarity, as with two neighbors discussing the accident while one discovers that the other has an unnervingly ghoulish interest in the injuries incurred.

One continuation of this etude is exploring what was revealed by each level of familiarity. For example, what do the familiarity levels show about the speakers, their relationship, and their sense of the event? What do the familiarity levels reveal about the characters' sense of place? What discoveries occur between the characters about their familiarity?

Variations

Show one relationship in a progression of familiarities: a couple meet in low-familiarity at an event (say they're followers of some long-running musical act like Dead Heads or Sinatra fans), become friends, encounter each other again in middle-familiarity at a similar event, and then marry and attend a third such occasion but now in high-familiarity. What would these different familiarities reveal about the progression of the relationship and the relationship's connection to the event?

Or give yourself a fact to reveal that is key to a plot (the recently purchased motel is haunted, for instance). Next, use the three different familiarities in separate scenes to reveal the fact. How does each familiarity change the way in which the information is revealed?

Some other variations: decide on the opening scene of a play—on the crucial event of that scene—then try the scene in the three different familiarities to see which one best delivers the quality you want at the outset of the play. Take a scene already written in one familiarity and rewrite it in another by changing either the basic relationship between the characters or by replacing one character.

SEE ALSO: Age Explorations, Best Friend, Character Collaboration, Dialogue Collaboration, Exposition Game, Filling in the Front, Spoken Subtext, and Status Etude.

Film Game

This is a variant of the Silent Movie etude. Though you are still going from one medium to another for the purpose of examining the effectiveness of your work on the stage, you now have sound available as a tool.

The Etude

Rewrite a scene from an existing play into a movie scene. Be sure to take advantage of the differences in the media—in film you have a choice of a variety of locations, different camera angles, and so on. By adhering strongly to film style, you will be able to get a new perspective on the style and choices of the original material. If you haven't read the Adaptation etudes, particularly Silent Movie, you should do so before continuing with this exercise to get a deeper background.

Although this is technically another Adaptation etude, I didn't lump it in with those because it's less narrow in structure. Silent Movie imposes a very severe restraint because you no longer have sound available; with Film Game, you can tell your story using many of the same tools you'd work with on stage. The discipline here is based on comparing expressive choices in different media, which is a bit more general.

The action of the scene won't change. What will be different is the mode of expression. While theatre is a very broad sensory experience, film is more focused. In theatre the audience has a lot of choices about where to look and how to listen. In film, those choices are more limited and manipulated. This manipulation (controlling where the audience looks and when and pushing their emotional buttons through images and sounds) has both positive and odious sides, but playwrights need to be aware of these differences.

Film relies largely on images. When I teach screenwriting I always exhort my students to pretend they're writing for people who cannot hear because this leads them more directly to film's natural asset: the telling of a story through sight. Yes, sound plays a large part in modern film but talk is still a smaller part of most films than image. This element alone will challenge the quality of your play's dialogue and show you how to make more of less. It is also going to challenge your use of images and teach you a great deal about not only the choice of images, but the choice of the sequence and juxtaposition of images as well.

Keep in mind as well that film generally requires a continual shifting of locale. Your play might be set in one place but your film adaptation of it probably shouldn't be, at least not for the exercise. This is where the Film Game meets the Place Exploration etudes: you are imposing variations on your scene's givens in order to see what impact those variations will have. This might lead you to open the original play to other locales, or it may convince you that a single locale is still best.

Variations

Write an original film scene rather than adapting a theatrical one, and then adapt it the other way. Or watch a film on video, select a sequence, rewatch this sequence, and then try to write it from memory. The point of this exercise would be to challenge your ability to see and recall and to question your own understanding of how the film's sequence worked.

SEE ALSO: Adaptation Etudes, Adapting to the Stage Etudes, Film Reversal, Mystery Imposition, and Place Explorations.

Film Reversal

This etude forces you to deal as creatively as you can with the elements of the stage to solve a problem opposite from those presented by Film Game or Silent Movie. There are similar exercises in Chapter 6 called the Adapting to the Stage Etudes that are more focused on plot concerns than technique, but they will be worth your time to try in conjunction with this etude.

The Etude

Take the published screenplay of a film you really love and adapt a sequence from the film for the stage. Choose a sequence that will be challenging because it works naturally in film (like a runaway wagon scene in a Western or a space battle from a science fiction movie) but presents enormous challenges for the stage. Limit yourself to the creative capabilities of actors and the use of standard stage devices and avoid film, video, or other high-tech equipment to make the work easy. Be sure to stay as faithful as you can to the spirit and perspective of the original film scene.

I once directed a play called *Gorilla* by John Patrick Shanley in which there was a boat chase—a cop chasing a boatload of monkeys in a Central Park lake. This was at the Dorset Theatre Festival in Vermont, and budgets have never permitted high-tech solutions there. We tried putting the boats on wheels and pulling them about the stage but they were heavy and awkward and kept going out of control—especially since we had a raked stage. The simple solution was to have the actors playing the monkeys carry a bottomless boat while the cop "wore" his little boat with a pair of heavy-duty suspenders. It actually made the scene much funnier, I think, than a solution involving elaborate technical devices to create something more "real."

Don't limit your thinking here to action-adventure films, and avoid films already confined to theatrical-type locations. The job of this etude is to find new ways of giving life and imagination to ideas that have already been successfully expressed in another medium. The point of eliminating high-tech stuff is to ask you to rely on the tools that can be made more creative by the human touch. While I'm not anti-tech, elaborate technology is too often substituted for more creative responses.

Consider as well how you might put Hitchcock's *Rear Window* on stage. It is, after all, a film made entirely on a studio set, with no extra locations needed and mostly from one point of view. Could you make it work in a theatre? See the movie if you never have, and then give it a whirl. Have fun.

SEE ALSO: Adaptation Etudes, Adapting to the Stage Etudes, Film Game, and Place Explorations.

Place Exploration 1

This etude explores the impact a particular place will have on character or plot. The focus of Place Exploration 1 is on an original piece; the focus of 2 is on reexploring an existing piece; the focus of 3 is on place-as-mood.

Place has a huge impact on our lives. If it didn't, we'd just take our vacations in our workplace rather than at the beach or in the country, and we'd never bother to decorate our homes. Place also has a massive impact on our plays. Think about a character with a monologue about who to vote for set in a country that completely oppresses its citizens. Or consider how a rather vapid speech such as "The sunset tonight is like my heart" (see the Problem-Solving Monologue etude) might change if it was being spoken by someone dying in a collapsed mine shaft.

The Etude

Create a scene in which the action is dependent on the nature of the place in which the scene is set. Keep in mind for postanalysis that you were exploring a place, your characters' reactions to this place, and the impact of the place on the shape of the plot all at the same time. Start by choosing a series of places that have very specific resonances for you. These can be real or simply locations that trigger an emotional response in you.

This etude gives you a lot of possibilities for exploring plot or character before writing a play because you can test your characters in such a variety of locales. By putting characters in places where they will have to have strong positive or negative reactions, you will discover much about their spirit, reactions, and ethics. You could include locations that are extremely dangerous (a war zone or a mountain top), extremely comfortable (an ideal beach or spa), or which in some way takes a character out of the "normal" setting (e.g., putting a city kid on a farm). Try to allow the situation to be intrinsically based on place rather than environment (see the Environmental Exploration etude) so that the character has to deal with things specific to that place. This might necessitate research to make the writing about the place more accurate, and such research might open up other possibilities for this play or future plays.

This etude's potentials for plot exploration expands in several directions. Simply seeing where characters have the most interesting reactions is especially worthwhile if you have characters who intrigue you but no plot to put them in. Perhaps you even have characters from another play you'd like to reexplore. Another direction might be evolving plot ideas specifically from a choice of place and letting a given place evoke possibilities for you. Ponder choices such as a Tibetan temple or a traffic jam on the Brooklyn Bridge.

SEE ALSO: Age Explorations, Being There Etudes, Disaster, Environmental Exploration, Ground Plan Collaboration, Place Explorations, and Where Do I Live?

Place Exploration 2

This variation is somewhat more plot oriented than Place Exploration 1 because this etude is focused on reexploring an existing play rather than on developing a new one. However, rewriting or adapting always affect character, and you'll need to stay open to the changes this exploration may bring to your characters and the plot.

The Etude

Choose a scene that you feel is not working or needs to be rethought. Rewrite the scene by placing the characters in a completely different environment than that of the extant play. What happens to your story and characters because of this new location? As with any other etude that reworks an existing piece, you may find you'll want to incorporate some or all of the new discoveries into the old material, or you may just chuck out the new altogether. The crux is taking another look at your material in a nonintellectual and nonlinear fashion.

You can pick a new location that would be a logical alternate locale from the current setting (i.e., her place instead of his). Or you could choose a locale that would be illogical and would therefore influence the characters in a very different way, such as relocating the scene to a desert or under the ocean. Another possibility would be to place the rewrite in a completely unreal environment such as Mars, Hell, or someone's stomach.

Use this etude to play with your characters and story away from the familiar locales of your original piece. It will help you to see what their behavior might be in other places, and it will benefit your thinking about the quality of the locales you've chosen for your play.

A caveat goes with this etude, however: try to keep the overall objectives of your characters intact while you explore this other place. The easiest way to get lost here is to let everything change just because of place, but the real point is to see how a new place will alter the dynamics of a given scene. You may, of course, have a scene that's basically dead in the water, in which case changing the place should change everything. Trust your impulses here.

In fact, this etude also has real potential for someone who's blocked with a particular scene or play. It will allow you to develop the scene while staying away from forcing the original scene to work. Sometimes, after all, what you have is a nice, simple dough-nut, and trying to pound it into being a croissant only creates enormous frustration. Allowing yourself the freedom of placing the scene anywhere else gives you room to breathe and—perhaps—enough perspective to discover what the scene really is about and where it needs to go.

SEE ALSO: Age Explorations, Being There Etudes, Disaster, Environmental Exploration, Ground Plan Collaboration, Place Explorations, and Where Do I Live?

Place Exploration 3

This is a narrower variation on the previous Place etudes. It entails choosing a place with an emphatic mood or impact, such as a funeral parlor or a disco. The etude may be used either for original exploration or reworking an existing piece, and you can use it to work on character and/or plot.

The Etude

The key difference between this etude and the other two Place etudes is imposing the element of mood on a scene. Write or rewrite a scene by choosing a place you feel has a strong inherent mood attached to it. Trust your own instincts here as to defining "mood." For instance, where I might find a mountain top an exhilarating place, your reaction might be one of fear—it's your choice that matters. By the same token, pay close attention to the reactions of your characters when they're introduced to this place-as-mood because their reactions might be quite at variance from yours. Also, be very careful to incorporate as many specifics about the mood of the place as possible into your exploration.

Think about a place that's basically organized for dancing. A honky-tonk or Roseland is usually a noisy place where people are having a lot of fun. But this doesn't mean there aren't people who are having a lousy time. In fact, I've personally had some of my most miserable times in such places simply because they strained me toward such shrill cheer. By choosing a place with a strong mood potential, you can allow your characters a great deal of reaction room. You also have the additional asset of knowing that your audience will have a pretty automatic connection to the locale, which gives you other factors to play with like running the scene counter to expectations (e.g., a character who cannot stop bursting into laughter during a wedding).

You might want to make a list of places with given moods to allow yourself some fun variations to play with. I chose a funeral parlor and a disco because they're places where most of us have had some experience, but there are myriad possibilities. The main thing is to give yourself a place to play that will be entertaining, challenging, and even surprising.

SEE ALSO: Age Explorations, Being There Etudes, Disaster, Environmental Exploration, Ground Plan Collaboration, Place Explorations, and Where Do I Live?

Problem-Solving Monologue

In this etude, your focus will be on writing a particular kind of monologue as an exploration. Before getting into specifics, however, I want to discuss some of the pitfalls of monologues.

I generally try to steer students away from monologues because they are often play-stoppers, especially descriptive monologues such as "I remember" interludes or speeches that melt into icky lyricism like "The sunset tonight is like my heart." To me, such monologues are like songs from a bad musical that have wandered into a straight show by accident. My personal choice always would be to show what's being said if it's so crucial: do the flashback or put the sunset on stage. Of course, the descriptive monologue has its place. The Greeks obviously made effective use of the technique, but their purpose was to provide crucial information and not just to write pretty speeches. In other words, if you must write an "I remember" or an "I saw this" speech, keep it short, to the point, and (above all) lose the adjectives.

Another plot-stopper is predictable pattern. I've noticed a particular kind of pattern after years of script-reading: several pages of dialogue will be followed by a monologue in which we're told what one of the characters really meant or in which we're retold what just happened. Several more pages of dialogue follow, which are again concluded with yet another monologue. This is a very weak use of the monologue form and should be avoided at all costs unless you've mastered your technique sufficiently to pull it off.

I'm using the term *monologue* here broadly to refer to a dramatic situation in which a character speaks without interruption to another character, an imaginary listener, the audience, or herself for an extended period. The form I tend to use the most is having a character talk directly to the audience, but only when I've decided the character needs to form a personal bond with the audience, and/or because I want the audience to feel part of the action. However, I generally try to avoid monologues in the context of a play. To me, the best use is outside the play for character exploration. The essence of the Problem-Solving Monologue etude is that kind of exploration.

The problem-solving monologue provides the character a conflict—often between two sides of herself—to work out. This is far more interesting and dramatic because it makes us wonder how the problem being discussed will be resolved and it engages us dramatically. A famous example of such a monologue is the "To be or not to be" soliloquy, which is essentially a kid saying, "Should I kill myself or not?"

The monologue should introduce a dilemma and then work to resolve it. Note that it's not necessary to come to a solution. I refer to problem solving only because I want the writer to actively work toward a solution on behalf of the character, but it's the pursuit that matters, not arriving someplace.

The Etude

Choose a character you're interested in exploring and give her a problem to talk about. This problem can be arbitrarily drawn just for the sheer fun of it or it can be a problem that you choose more deliberately because you expect it to reveal something specific about the character. Keep in mind that you want to discover the issue and/or solutions with the character and not for them. This etude is about voice and perspective because it is primarily a character study.

I often start working on my plays with problem-solving monologues for all of the characters because it allows me to see how they talk and reason, how honest they are, and how far they're willing to go for a solution. These monologues generally are not about a problem in the play but a problem in the character's life that lets me generate the kind of background and foundation exploration I need. In fact, I will frequently do whole sets of problem-solving monologues for each character just to see how they react to a variety of situations.

The problem-solving monologue can be used for a variety of other applications as well. You might practice "muscular" monologue writing. After all, anybody can write pages, but can you get your character's point across in half a page or less? Then again, if you can make the point in even less space, do you need the monologue at all? When in doubt, cut.

You could also aim the problem-solving directly at the play by letting a character articulate her perspective on solving an issue in the play. It's crucial, however, that you treat this as an exploration rather than trying to force the outcome by planning to incorporate the exercise into the play. Allow the character to assert her own voice and point of view; if that happens to work for the play as well, then great. If not, then it's no big loss. It would even be fun, particularly if you're having a rough time with a piece, to have a character discuss the play itself in a problem-solving monologue—"This is what I think is wrong with this stinking play!" (See also an etude in Chapter 9 called They're Talking About You.)

For an existing play, turn a remembrance or descriptive monologue you've already written into a problem-solving monologue. Do this by creating a conflict within the character that gives the formerly passive voice a more active pursuit. For instance, an argument with oneself over the accuracy of a memory—"Was it a Tuesday or a Wednesday? Albany? Rochester?"—becomes automatically more engaging because there's something at stake. You could also learn a great deal by writing a monologue in which what the speaker is trying to describe nearly defies description, such as a moment of horror or great revelation. Lastly you might work to turn a descriptive monologue from something with a nostalgic or romantic tone into something more troubled and/or rooted in a nonsentimental reality. This might necessitate having the character speak at different emotional times—during the crying, just after the crying is over, or a day later when a cooler reality has set in.

Regardless of how you pursue this etude, I want to conclude as I started: try not to use monologues in your plays. It's true that there are many plays with brilliant monologues in them—and some plays that are just monologues like Brian Friel's magnificent *The Faith Healer*—but there are far more plays that are undone by sappy and pointless speeches. In the end, the same questions apply to everything you put into your play. Is this necessary? Does it engage the audience dramatically? Does it move the play forward? While the monologue form has great potential for exploration, as a dramatic element it has enormous problems.

Variations

Write a monologue that focuses on the problem the speaker is having with another character rather than an internal difficulty. You could also extend this situation by having two or more characters privately voice their problems with each other.

SEE ALSO: Age Explorations, Disaster, Oral History, and They're Talking About You.

Secret Behavior

This etude is based on an acting exercise called the Private Moment. The actor is asked to recreate her home environment with some personal props and then occupy that environment in as private a way as possible in front of the acting class or workshop. The aim of the exercise is to lead to behavior that one would probably stop if intruded on, such as dancing like Baryshnikov in your pajamas, singing like your favorite singer into your hairbrush, or being undressed. The purpose of the Private Moment is to free the actor from inhibitions about revealing private behavior in public, which is extremely important since "being private in public" is one definition of the actor's craft. Once the actor has done this exercise a few times, playing a character whose behavior or values feel unnatural to the actor becomes less of a problem, as does revealing emotions the actor might have previously found to be difficult to express.

The Etude

The Secret Behavior etude is based on the Private Moment in several ways. First, the etude may be written exactly like a Private

Moment with a character (or characters) in a situation that is very private, personal, and/or potentially embarrassing—activity they'd be very likely to stop if an outsider intruded—and then you create the intrusion. This allows you to see the reactions of your characters to such an invasion and explore their privacy.

This exploration of privacy allows you to create a texture in your characters you might not have otherwise. I strongly recommend this etude as a developmental point in creating characters for a play because it allows you to examine their secret worlds. This might lead to personality aspects you'll want to include in the play, or it might simply remain an exploration, but you will know your character.

Why have I included this etude in the chapter on technique rather than in the chapter on character? Because this is an etude that can provide important craft growth: you are putting your characters (and your own creative impulses as well) at risk in pretty much the same way an actor does for the Private Moment. As with all the etudes, a vital element to making the best use of this process is paying attention to the choices you make intuitively in doing the exercises.

For example, let's say you have a character engaging in Secret Behavior that relates to a food compulsion (I remember an acting student who almost always had a cake or some fattening food hidden away for their private moment exercises). What this tells you about the character is important of course, but even more useful is what this tells you about your view of the character and of yourself. That is to say, what's your personal relationship with food?

When I smoked, many of the characters in my plays also smoked. Now that I'm a rabidly nonsmoking antismoker, I only have a character smoke in a play if I think it really makes a huge difference to that character. My interest is in the nature of these choices and how they reflect both my characters and myself. Many people are very resistant to this kind of psychological perspective and analysis. I can certainly understand their wariness and so I offer my thoughts as a strictly take-it-or-leave-it proposition. My main argument is that craft excellence comes from an awareness of process in terms of how we work and who we are as we work.

Regardless, the Secret Behavior etude gives you a vital tool for exploring the psychology of your characters—what secrets and fears and private joys you give them helps create the fullest possible tapestry of their personality, which will in turn help bring the largest life to the stage. Consider, for instance, the character of Salieri in *Amadeus*: try to imagine him without his sweets obsession. Now go the next step and see how much the absence of the sweets obsession as a metaphor would harm the texture of the play. Consider as well what the difference would be if Peter Shaffer's version of Mozart were not so sexually obsessed or so childish in his obsessions. Perhaps not every play requires these kinds of private behavior elements, but *Amadeus* is clearly a superior play for their inclusion.

Variations

Put two characters on stage in a situation in which one has a secret she is actively trying to keep from the other. You might have a drunk teenager trying to sneak in past her father, for instance. Remember to keep this focused on behavior. How many ways can you find for the character with the secret to keep it, and how will the other character react to this behavior? Or put both characters on stage with secrets. Of course, the inclination might be to rewrite O'Henry's "Gift of the Magi," but there are many other directions in which one could go with this variation.

In these variations, a very important decision is when the behavior will lead to dialogue, if it should at all (see the etude called Behavior to Inevitable Words). One obvious choice would be starting when the secret is revealed so you would explore how behavior changes once one character's secret is known to the other. Another direction would result if what a character thinks she knows about the secret isn't exactly right. And a fun extension would be an exploration of whether the person with the secret knows she has been found out or not. It's possible that a whole play could be built just on the continuing complications based on a single secret.

SEE ALSO: Behavior to Inevitable Words, Best Friend, Familiarity Etude, Personal Problem, Secret Objective, Secret Past, Situation Exploration, and Stage Directions Only.

Secret Objective

This etude is similar to Secret Behavior except that it has a far more specific purpose and the results should be quite different.

Revealing secret objectives in characters is an extremely important technique for playwrights to master simply because it gives you the ability to deal in characters and plots that are multi-leveled and complex.

The Etude

Write a scene in which one of the characters has a secret objective—you could also think of it as a hidden agenda—which it is your task to reveal during the course of the scene. The real test is to see how you can reveal the secret objective through implication because you must never state it directly. The technique to learn is how to get information across in the most subtle manner possible.

Suppose a character has a secret desire to be the chief power figure in a business. She might not be able to openly show this desire, but the audience will see her working in the background to attain it. Meanwhile, this character might show a completely trustworthy persona to the other characters. The dynamic of these two faces makes for good theatre because it adds a layer to the conflict of the play, and adds texture to the character. Now, not all secret objectives have to be dark. I remember a friend telling me once that because he was so overweight as a child he wanted to be invisible; so he practiced stealing from room to room as silently as possible to create the effect. His secret objective would be to be light as air or to be invisible.

There are two crucial aspects to this exercise: making choices as to who needs to perceive this secret objective, and understanding that it's not the secretive character's job to reveal the hidden agenda but yours.

Choosing who needs to perceive this information is critical in this etude and in your plays. Your options are the other character(s) in the scene and the audience. What the other character comprehends may or may not be the issue, but what the audience comprehends will always be the issue. In other words, it may not be vital to the scene whether the other character comprehends, but it is extremely important that the audience understands and how it understands. Many playwrights don't entirely trust the audience to get it, so they have a tendency to really lather up the point when there's a key element to get across. This tends to make the audience passive because information is being spoonfed, and it can turn an audience off entirely if they recognize condescension at work. This etude is a strong study in the necessary techniques to effectively suggest critical information.

The second crucial element of this etude is the really fun part again because it isn't the character-with-the-secret's job to reveal her secret, but the playwright's. It's far more interesting if this character's secret is revealed inadvertently, in fact. You may have a character who has a need to reveal this secret objective—Iago reveling in his duplicity, for instance—and that would be acceptable of course, but it's rather rare. Most of the time, the revealing of a secret objective seems accidental but is part of the playwright's palette for that particular character and play. This ties into the first element above because you must reveal the secret objective subtly, and you must determine when it needs to be revealed.

For instance, I wrote a one-act play in which a character wants some letters belonging to someone else. In early drafts I didn't make this clear enough for the dynamic of the play because I let the information out very late in the plot. I didn't know how to put the element in earlier because it was the crucial element of the plot. Another playwright finally suggested that I should have the character seen onstage at the beginning of the play searching through a bureau without the other character knowing it (she was offstage taking a shower). This turned out to be the perfect solution because the audience knew the guy was after something but it didn't know what. Plus, the audience could watch the same play that had originally seemed flat and perceive the action as very charged because it was in on the deal.

I also like Secret Objective as an etude and as a playwriting practice because it's rooted in some really potent aspects of theatre. It reminds us that our job as playwrights is not to tell a story so much as to show a story. This approach lets the audience be active because the members are piecing together our hints and suggestions to create a whole. It also reminds us that the essence of theatre is watching other humans—spying on them, if you will, through that fourth wall—and letting our fascination with their behavior go completely free.

Variations

Give both characters in a scene a secret objective or even the same secret objective. A different approach would be to put one character in a situation in which she has to reveal her hidden agenda but either doesn't want to or is dying to. You could also create a basic scene as a template, and then change the hidden agenda each time, just to see what effect the change has over the entire scene. In other words, what would the difference be if the secret agenda was to get ten dollars from Leslie as opposed to trying to get Leslie to lie in court? This etude has a multitude of possibilities. I encourage you to play with it in as many ways as you can think of.

SEE ALSO: Behavior to Inevitable Words, Best Friend, Familiarity Etude, Personal Problem, Secret Objective, Secret Past, Situation Exploration, and Stage Directions Only.

Vocal Distinctions

Far too many scripts I encounter have characters who all speak with the same rhythms and word choices. Some of this I attribute to the homogenization of the American culture due to cable and satellite TV access, but some of it is just lazy writing.

When I first got going as a writer, my immediate impulse was to copy the people in the Writers' Bloc whose work I admired. The problem was I couldn't hack it. They were younger, urban, differently ethnic from anything I'd known, and their style just wasn't me. My breakthrough came when I started on a piece set in Baltimore, my home town, and used its very odd dialect, rhythm, and slang. Once I started giving characters from Baltimore their true voices, my writing got better and the textures of the characters became much richer.

Vocal Distinctions is a catch-phrase here for a broad range of exercises having to do with developing more awareness and appreciation of the vast differences in expression that exist around us. This would include such elements as regional dialects, rhythms, slang, choice of obscenities, and so on.

The Etude

Decide on two characters who speak differently from one another in unique ways due to dialects, rhythms, slang, and so on. Now put them in a scene together. The obvious choice of scene would be having the two attempt to understand one another, but there are a thousand other ways so don't settle for the obvious. For instance, consider having two characters with opposite dialects (Brooklyn and Mississippi) sniping at each other as opposing lawyers, disputing a fact about the Civil War, trying to agree on a presidential candidate, or settling on where to have lunch.

Keep in mind that the mode of expression reveals the way of thinking and doesn't necessarily limit how the character thinks. Most of my students in New York tended to write or improvise southern dialect with characters who just had to be stupid. My students in El Paso often think that everybody in New York sounds like Kojak. If you think this way, your head is cluttered with clichés and needs a vacuuming—serious research, such as actually meeting people from other locales and ethnicities, will do wonders for you.

I don't recommend writing in dialect for your plays (it's very hard for actors to work with—try reading *Pygmalion* sometime if you want a quick lesson). My suggestion would be to specify the locality of the dialect and/or write just a few early lines in the dialect to give the flavor and hope you get conscientious actors who will do the necessary homework to create the proper sounds. For the exercise, however, I do recommend writing entirely in dialect because it'll be more like writing a musical score for your own benefit. The look of the words on the page alone will be valuable for your analysis of the exercise. Keep in mind as well that it's not only dialect that distinguishes us—word choices (which is the issue of the next etude) of all kinds make us specific and unique, as do vocal distinctions that are physical in nature. Consider a very loud talker or a person inclined to lisp or mumble.

Variations

Rewrite an existing scene using one or more kinds of vocal distinctions as the focus of the rewrite. You might leave character A exactly the same but change character B's dialogue into dialect just to see what impact this has on the scene. It may not change the meaning of the scene, but it will definitely change the texture, and that's worth looking at anytime. You might then rewrite the same scene and change character A instead of B to see where that takes you. You could also write or rewrite a scene in which all the characters speak exactly alike to see the effect or frame the scene around the fact that nobody speaks alike in any way.

There are numerous ways of pursuing this same basic etude. The main thing for you to consider is how to apply it. Do your characters sound so alike they're interchangeable? Is that your point?

How can you find ways to make them more distinct from one another? Can you do this without making the characters into clichés? The answer may not lie in making one of them talk like Gomer Pyle but may be found in more subtle distinctions.

SEE ALSO: Best Friend, Cross-Cultural Etude, Dialogue Collaboration, Familiarity Etude, Normal Day, Oral History, Problem-Solving Monologue, Spoken Subtext, Status Etude, Style Copy, Where Do I Live?, and Word Choice.

Word Choice

This is a very useful etude. It can be done with an original piece or as a way of taking a new look at an existing play. The basic exercise here is based on the making of extremely precise word choices in a given scene (which ought to be done routinely, anyway).

Here's a simple example: What is our natural assumption when somebody starts complimenting us on our looks, clothes, or hair? One assumption might be that the complimentor is being very nice. Another might be that this person is hitting on us. A third might be that the complimentor is looking for a compliment in return and hoping to draw attention to something new or unusual about herself. The key to understanding will be in the language. If she's hitting on someone, the word choices should reveal a romantic or sexual interest beneath the seemingly casual compliments. If she's fishing for compliments, the word choices should be more self-reflexive (or possibly self-denigrating, depending on the character). Regardless, the issue is the layering of the motive(s) behind the words as revealed in the choice of words.

This is a real nuts-and-bolts etude because word choice is a critical aspect of your plays. So much can be revealed with a single word—provided the choice has been made very carefully by the playwright. You'll find that word choice is a crucial element of many other etudes as well.

It should be said that intonation can play a part in how any words get said on stage; however, the choice of the exactly right word will create that intonation rather than leaving it up to the actor. In this fashion, the playwright creates a collaboration with the actor, giving her words from which to launch objectives and meanings.

The Etude

If you're trying this etude with original material, start by creating a scene in which the word choices are all very carefully selected to convey a secret objective (which is an etude to look at if you haven't). You might try another original piece based on giving one character a particular motive for word choice, such as an over-achiever who's trying out new vocabulary words on everyone. A third original piece might be trying the complimenting variations I suggested above or something comparable.

If you're trying this etude with an existing piece, the game is to change the word choices in every line to make them stronger. In other words, if someone refers to another's clothing as "hot," what would happen if they referred to the clothing instead as "blazing" or "incendiary"? Or if they wanted to insult, what if they mentioned "ashes" or wondered if the clothes came "from a fire sale"? Obviously, a choice will depend on your decisions for the character and on your range of vocabulary. Unearth your thesaurus if you haven't already.

There are endless variations on this etude, all based on the concept of playing with word choice to reveal character and/or intention. Other kinds of word choices would include having characters use too many or too few words; adding words or phrases that particularize the character (in my old neighborhood in Baltimore, many people added "ain't it?" to everything they said as the local equivalent of "right?"); or punctuating a character's dialogue with words like obscenities that might seem inappropriate but reveal a hidden layer to the character's mental state (constant scatological references might reveal a bowel obsession or problem).

SEE ALSO: Best Friend, Cross-Cultural Etude, Dialogue Collaboration, Familiarity Etude, Normal Day, Oral History, Problem-Solving Monologue, Spoken Subtext, Status Etude, Style Copy, Where Do I Live?, and Vocal Distinctions.

Writing Lyrics

This is a fun exercise for opening up your intuitive response to other artists and for expanding your technical range.

The Etude

Choose a song without lyrics and write lyrics to it. The purpose is to try to capture both the rhythm and emotion of the purely abstract music with your words. Try writing different lyrics to the same tune on different days—force yourself to rethink your first response to the meaning of the tune and to seek out variations on what you hear. I've done this with students with tunes like "Flying" by the Beatles, the instrumental opening of "The Stranger" by Billy Joel, or "Pretty Little Ditty" by the Red Hot Chili Peppers. I try to stay in the realm of pop music for my students' benefit. Other music forms are fine, but you'll probably want to avoid any that go off too erratically or that have too complex a structure. The point is to develop lyrics based on a very simple tune and not to leap in as if you're Richard Wagner.

This will work with any melody you choose, however, so long as it's not already too familiar or connected to a meaning you could not deviate from. In the age of Karaoke, you could provide yourself with a number of tunes without words that you might not be familiar with. However, in all cases you should try not to know the title of the piece you've chosen.

Variations

Use this as a character exploration: what lyrics would a given character make up to the tune you've selected? You could also go another step and have the character make up the tune and all—I'm thinking of the fascinating songs the actors wrote for their characters in Robert Altman's film *Nashville*.

What you can derive from this etude is a lot of technical awareness and expertise you might not have realized before. It might not turn you into a lyricist but it will certainly open your intuitive channels. Lastly, this is an excellent option for a blocked writer (see Chapter 9 for more on this), and it gives you something to write that requires no particular result or application. Call it a crossword puzzle for stumped creativity.

SEE ALSO: Composing to Music, Games, Other Forms, Style Copy, and Word Choice.

5

CHAPTER

Character Etudes

NOW THAT YOUR MUSCLES ARE NICELY BUILT UP FROM THE technique etudes, it's time to apply them to something. Why should you look at character before plot? Partly because it's my opinion that we're writing weakish characters these days, and partly because character is at the center of theatre. After all, we don't usually talk about some Danish kid who's got a ton of problems. We just mention Hamlet and most people know who that is and what his story was. And we don't refer to the "guy-who-killed-his-father-and-married-his-mother complex"—we apply a person's name to it because the essence is human.

This is not to deny plot's critical role. Where are we, after all, without a story? But my argument will remain that it is the theatre's primary function and joy to examine the human condition above all other things.

There are some plays that are far more dependent on plot than character, of course, but the audience will always need some way to connect with or be distanced from the story, which is always accomplished through character. Distancing, for example, often needs to occur in experimental pieces, where the images or the philosophy are more important than a linear plot. In this situation, the characters are intentionally made inaccessible, stereotypical, or imagistic. But, character choices have indeed been made, and a characterization of some kind has been crafted. Even when a play is totally plot oriented, characters exist because the audience needs to find itself in the material in some way. A play without any characters—a piece with vacuum cleaners as characters, for example—is still defined by character because we understand it by measuring the absence of humans.

Movies have shown us the danger of ignoring character for the sake of plot. Action-adventure films tend to sketch the main characters in quick strokes so we can get on with the carnage. Most such films rely on a star whose name alone evokes the character's necessary qualities: cold, with a one-track mind, casually carnal, destructive, jingoistic, and muscularly exaggerated. These characters often have to be non- or superhuman in order to make the degree of potential carnage even greater. In other words, even the "heroes" have become weapons. It's necessary in this genre to limit the humanity of all the characters because humanity just gets in the way and brings us back to the worst of melodrama. The characters may have names but their real identities are "mindlessly violent villain," "cannon-fodder antagonist," "sex object female," "obsessive hero-type," and so on.

Is this the direction we want for theatre? I won't try to argue with people who will point out the immense popularity of these movies. History has shown us all too well that the dollar is almighty. I'm only arguing with people who are still wonderfully foolish enough to want to talk about art and theatre, in particular. I thus pose this question: Do we want the stage to become a place where scenery and effect are more important than character?

Assuming the answer is a resounding no, that leaves us, the brave scouts of the theatre, hacking our way through the remaining wilderness. Let's consider that image for a moment. To comfort ourselves in the dark nights, we tell stories around the campfire like our ancestors did for thousands of years. What if in the telling we say, "This is about anybody at all, who one day happened to find a rare stone . . ."? Why does that seem so weak? Because we obviously need to talk about a character, a specific person whose actions give us courage in the dark, provide inspiration, or scare the pants off us. In the long run it doesn't matter if he found a rare stone, swept out a stable, or even cut throats for revenge and culinary processing. What does matter is that we enter this world and understand it through another human being. And that's the main connector.

I teach the notion that virtually every play has at least one character through whom we enter the play. It might be as direct as Alfieri in A *View from the Bridge* or as indirect as the outsiders Vershinin and Natalya in *The Three Sisters*. The playwright needs to somehow find a character whose point of view lets us see into the world of the play like a peephole in an Easter egg. More often than not, it's the main character we're following and concerned about, but there are no hard and fast rules on this. The only thing for certain is that the character you want us to see the play through must be a credible human being in the context of the play. He is the one person we can rely on for a kind of true insight—no matter whether that insight is fair or unfair, sane or crazy—so we know where the parameters are in the world of the play.

Elements of character break down into various categories: physical qualities, mental capabilities, background, current occupation, current preoccupation, and so on. You can create your own categories and breakdowns, and the etudes that follow are designed to help you do this. They will also help you to discover things about your characters and let them give expression to these things (and you may create your own etudes to answer your own needs). What I've tried to do is compile a group of exercises I've found useful and fun. These may be used for initial exploration or to intensify and texturize characters from an existing play.

The key etude is Age Exploration. It has three major variations, all based on qualities such as discovering character choices, tastes, and mental states using age as a primary factor. The Age Exploration etudes are derived from some of Viola Spolin's games concerning who the character is and from some basic concepts I learned from teachers I've been trained by or observed.

The "who" games and exercises in Spolin's books concern exploring character choices actively through a variety of circumstances. Her work forms the basis of many of the etudes here and in the Technique Etudes. The fact that a character must have a unique identity is fairly obvious, and these etudes are helpful for discovering a variety of unique attributes.

The basic concepts I've learned from teachers are a bit more complex. The first is a loose rule of thumb used in a sensory exercise called a Sense Memory. The nature of this exercise is to go back into your own personal history and recall a particular moment through your senses, usually one that is very strong emotionally. You should remember what you saw, smelled, tasted, and so on. The rule was stated: choose a moment from a time that is at least seven years ago. When I asked why seven years, I was told that, theoretically, the body renews itself every seven years, and so does the mind in the sense that by the time we've lived with something for at least seven years, we've matured enough to understand it. Twenty-one can finally begin to comprehend the turmoil of fourteen, while things that happened to you last year may still be too alive in your emotional landscape to cope with.

Whether this is scientifically true or not, I do think it's an important starting point for the key etude in this chapter because it suggests that both age and an understanding of age are vital to us and our characters. Whether you accept the notion of seven years as a renewal and perspective point or not, there are clearly typical age-related behaviors (we can expect a sixteen year old to be in rebellion of some kind), but age-related behaviors are specific to the perceptions, maturity, and experiences of each character and are not simple clichés (so the sixteen year old may not be in rebellion).

The other essential concept is that a character is only living a portion of his life in the time of the play. I touched on this already in Chapter 2 so I won't belabor it here. The point is that if it's the responsibility of the actor to create a more complete life for their character than exists in the script, then it is even more so the responsibility of the playwright. If we really take care of the details of our creations, the expressive capacity of our characters will be that much greater. The etudes in this chapter give you as full a range as I can think of—covering elements of personality, habitat, daily life, place in society, and more. Working through them diligently will provide you with a very broad palette of choices for your characters.

Lastly, since I've spoken in such detail about uniqueness, let me spend a moment on another element of character: universality. Universality is a literary term that we've come to fear and loathe because it's one of those gullet-stuffers (like that other bugaboo, theme) shoveled into us by well-meaning teachers and authors without clarifying what it is or how it exists in real life. Universality simply means that a character possesses a wide enough range of human qualities as to represent a spectrum of human beings. In other words, a one-armed man with a very limited IQ who came from the poorest family in the tiniest village in Tibet could share with us, in spite of all his otherwise unique differences, a love of his children, a sense of humor, and a reverence for the Earth. When we're biased, it's generally because we've gotten hung up on a particular and forgotten to connect with the universal about another person.

All characters do not have to be universal, but I would submit that a play in which all of the characters are as full-ranged as possible will be a stronger play. Of course, I assume that such a play warrants such characters—it may not be what you're trying to write, but even in that case it's the departure from universality that's critical.

In all cases, the issue will always be craft and technique. Do your characters just appear out of the ether or are you in control of their creation? Are they two-dimensional sketches or fully developed persons? The character etudes that follow will help address these and other questions.

KEY ETUDE
Age Exploration 1
This etude is for examining preexisting characters by placing them in a different period of their lives from the time of the play. For instance, if you're writing about a couple who are having a bad time of it in their marriage, go back and write about the marriage at its start or write about the relationship that existed before the marriage. The point of the exploration is to discover the qualities that made the relationship work at one point compared to what's preventing the relationship from working now. In doing so, you avoid clichés or superficial characterizations.

For instance, if a woman is divorcing a man, we often tend to assume infidelity and leave it at that, which is neither very interesting nor the only possibility. What if the infidelity was to a cause or to a religion instead of the typical affair? What if the infidelity was just in the woman's mind? What if? By exploring the stages of the relationship it's possible to create (or discover) the seeds of a conflict at an earlier time and allow those seeds to bloom into something unique, specific, and genuine.

The Etude

Reexplore an existing relationship between two characters (you can do more than two, but it's far more complicated) by writing scenes about earlier periods when the nature of the relationship was at odds with what it is now. This could include the earlier and happier, as suggested above; it could also include earlier and unhappier. Also, don't be too literal about the now versus then being strictly based on emotional states. For instance, you could explore an earlier relationship when a father was strong and his child was ill as an exploration for a play in which the father is now ill and the former child has become his caretaker.

It's essential to be as faithful to the ages of the characters as to the periods in which they are these ages. There's a lot of difference between sexual relationships, for instance, in 1959, 1969, and then in AIDS-era 1989. There's also a lot of difference between being eighteen, twenty-eight, and forty-eight. Make sure you deal with both age and era truthfully, and factually.

Variation

Try going into the future to explore the original relationship a year after the breakup. This gives you the chance to explore the aftermath and hindsight aspects—particularly of elements that the characters themselves may be surprised by (ranging from "I haven't missed you at all" to a revelation of deep regret). Harold Pinter's Betrayal is a terrific example of the Age Exploration etude's concept of looking at various ages and times as barometers in relationships.

Whether you go into the past or the future, this kind of exploration may provide you with material you can incorporate into the play itself. I always encourage writers to choose a flashback or flashforward scene over a more passive remembrance monologue in a play—what the audience gets to witness is almost always more theatrically engaging than what they are simply told.

SEE ALSO: Age Explorations, Best Friend, Disaster, Familiarity Etude, Flashbacks and Flashforwards, Other Era, Personal Problem, Personal Quality, and Secret Past.

Age Exploration 2

This version is for exploring characters at ages extremely different from their current age. It's important to understand that *extreme* is a word chosen more for the image it creates than for its literal meaning. Extreme could mean taking a character from being thirty to being three, but it could also mean going from twenty-five to being sixteen or from sixteen to seven. Nine years isn't much. Except at those particular ages.

The Etude

Explore characters at ages extremely different from their current age. This may be done with a new piece or to reexplore an existing play's characters. If you'd written *Hamlet*, for example, it would be fun to rewrite him at the age of five or, if he'd lived, at sixty or even one hundred. This gives you an opportunity to explore the differences in perspective that age may create. It might also be a way of discovering a time of trauma or great happiness you didn't know existed in the character's life. I've also thought it would be fascinating to write about a real person, like a horrible villain such as Hitler or Stalin when he was young and his mind turned toward the darker aspects of personality. Or to write a scene in which this person is very old and comes face to face finally with the horrors he perpetrated and engendered.

Variations

Change the ages of both characters in a scene. If the scene is an argument between a married couple, the quality of the argument at age forty and age six will obviously be quite different—or will it? The discovery here may very well be that your married couple actually fight like six year olds. Or rewrite a scene with the characters as if only one has changed age radically. This would have the grandmother of your play talking to her husband, except that he's fourteen now. Obviously, this would intensely alter the relationship, but the point is the exploration of the differences found in extreme ages. We've all probably fantasized about wanting to meet our parents or grandparents at younger ages—*Field of Dreams* is a perfect example of the potency of this fantasy—and giving your characters a chance to do it opens up all kinds of possibilities. Since you're a writer, giving yourself the opportunity to play with this, whether for your characters or for your own family or self has rich potential.

SEE ALSO: Age Explorations, Best Friend, Disaster, Familiarity Etude, Flashbacks and Flashforwards, Other Era, Personal Problem, Personal Quality, and Secret Past.

Age Exploration 3

The focus of this version is based on designating times in your character's life as key traumatic or problematic events. You should examine the personality of your character on the basis of his reactions to events that should be designed to provide you with some range of reaction. Examples include showing a character who was extremely ill at five, lost a parent at twelve, and was arrested for car theft at seventeen. The range of these events and the degree of their severity is entirely up to you. I used problematic or traumatic because a less-dire sequence might be braces at twelve, major pimple attack on the night of the prom, and an inability to purchase condoms at the local pharmacy at nineteen. The trick is to focus the events toward the current status or dilemma of the character you want to explore without overmanipulating.

The Etude

Explore a character during key events in his life. This may be done with a new character or with any of the population of a play already written. The purposes are various and might include creating a life story, crafting a problem history for your character, discovering the mindset of your character (how the present is affected by the past), or researching and exploring actual history that may have affected your character's life.

For example, if your character has to make a decision, you can write scenes that examine the time periods during which he experienced the major events that will lead to that decision. These periods may be real or fantasy, but you will get a decision that's really informed by the personal history and world view of the character much as your own choices are based on your life experience.

This is a fun etude because it asks that you try to write scenes from the crucial episodes of your character's life in order to discover what it was that led them to make a particular choice. For instance, a woman who is choosing not to accept a job might be doing so because of prior bad experiences in a similar situation, because she can't stand to be back in the same building where she was fired from her first job, or because she realizes she may have a problem with her potential boss.

This exploration is a creative acknowledgment that our past influences our present. The generation that went through the Depression tends to have different reactions to issues regarding politics, money, or social change than the generation that came of age during the 1960s. Knowing your character's personal history will be instructive to you; knowing that background in the larger context of social history will be even more helpful. This etude has enormous potential for plot applications as well because it creates a life history in a dramatic way. Rather than writing out a prose biography for your character, you are choosing instead to go back in time with them through a series of formative experiences.

Variations

Write scenes from your own life's key events to see how well you can capture the occurrences and what perspective you may have developed about them. If that's too close to home, you might try doing an oral history with someone (see the Oral History etudes) and attempt to script out that person's key events. As a further extension, you could also read some plays or see some films that have key past events as their basis—*Eleemosynary* by Lee Blessing, *Betrayal* by Harold Pinter, and *After the Fall* by Arthur Miller are some plays which come to mind. *Citizen Kane* is the main film that leaps out since it's structured precisely on key events and on perceptions of those events, but there are dozens of other movies that rely on similar formats.

A totally different take would be to utilize key events that are coming-of-age or levels-of-awareness steps. This could lead you, for instance, into phases of someone's maturity or through a sexual awakening.

A last variation would be to track several lives along key event paths that inevitably intersect. You would certainly do this if you had "star-crossed lovers" as your main characters, but numerous plot variations would work as well.

No matter how you choose to go with this etude, keep in mind that the whole point is the development of a full and textured life for your characters and the world they occupy. There are so many different kinds of milestones that mark our lives—be open to exploring a variety of possibilities.

SEE ALSO: Age Explorations, Best Friend, Disaster, Familiarity Etude, Flashbacks and Flashforwards, Other Era, Oral Histories, Personal Problem, Personal Quality, Problem-Solving Monologue, and Secret Past.

OTHER ETUDES
Best Friend
This is an excellent exercise for exploring a character who is under-developed or who is eluding you in some way.

The Etude
Give this troublesome character a confidant to talk with. This can be a best friend, sibling, therapist, bartender, or anyone else your instincts tell you the character could relate to in an intimate, open fashion. Write scenes that are away from the plot of the play so that you don't get trapped into script solutions. Keep in mind, however, that you do want to explore an aspect of the character that will apply to the play eventually, so stay in touch with your purpose. You could even have your character talk about the play itself to a friend, just as a way of breaking any limits on the character or plot you may have inadvertently imposed (see Chapter 9 for more on this approach).

Choosing a variety of situations will give you the widest range of results with this etude. For instance, talking to one's best friend in the afternoon is not quite the same as showing up at their door at three in the morning. Putting the two in a dire situation as in K–2 would open up a lot of possibilities as well. Your goal is to allow your character to explore feelings, dreams, secrets, and needs in a sufficient range of circumstances to really reveal the hidden layers.

As with all etudes, you should pay attention during your post-analysis of the exercise to your choice of friend for this character; the choice alone will tell you a great deal. And you should stay open to where things go between these characters—you may discover plots you hadn't considered. In fact, you may discover that the character you're exploring is just in the wrong play. You may discover that the friend of your character belongs in the play as well or even instead of your character. You must be very watchful in your creation of this confidant, particularly if the character is a therapist or other professional, to be certain that you're painting a fair and complete picture and not writing about a clichéd shrink. It is always useful to research and interview people in areas you're unfamiliar with rather than just drawing ideas from the air.

A nice twist would be to have the friend do most of the talking to examine your character as a listener and reactor. You may discover behavior for your character you never suspected. For example, if it's a phone call and your character is doodling, what does he doodle? People who draw endless boxes say one thing about themselves, while people who doodle clouds say quite another.

Variations

Have your character talk to a series of different confidants to see how he behaves in each situation. Have your character seek out a sequence of potential confidants with a particularly difficult issue that needs saying. Or have your character looking for a certain reinforcement through a sequence of people. You can also tie this exercise in with the Age Exploration etudes by setting the character and his confidant in different ages, levels of maturity, and so on.

SEE ALSO: Age Explorations, Character Collaboration, Normal Day, Other Attribute, Other Era, Personal Problem, Personal Quality, Secret Objective, Secret Past, and They're Talking About You.

Disaster

This is an extension of some etudes found in Chapter 4 (the Environmental Etude and Place Explorations), which are also excellent character etudes. In this version, the purpose is to explore a character's personality by placing him in the moments before, during, and following a disaster: how does he behave, who does he help or not, what does he save or not? I remember reading about Dustin Hoffman sometime in the late 1960s or early 1970s. He was talking about what happened when the house next to his exploded when some crazy bombers in the basement blew themselves up. As

I recall, he said that after having taken care to get his family out, he found himself on the street clutching a painting. He said he had no idea when or even why he grabbed the painting, but that's what his instincts told him to do at that moment.

Your choice of disaster—hurricane, drive-by shooting, or pimple outbreak—will obviously need to be related to the character you're working on. In what ways do you want to test this character's personality? Your choice could also impact on the plot this character occupies if you choose to incorporate elements of the disaster into your story.

The Etude

Working with a new or preexisting character, place this person in the way of a disaster of some kind. Your focus here should be on how the character behaves before (if there's any warning), during, and after the disaster occurs. You can instantly vary this scenario by having the impact of the disaster altered. In one exploration, the character sees the tornado coming, rushes to move his neighbor's family out of harm's way, gets them to safety. In a second exploration, the character doesn't get the family to safety. In the third, the character gets them to safety but is badly injured himself. Keep going until you feel you've really exhausted the possibilities.

Variations

There are innumerable variations on this single etude. Look for ways of testing your character that will reveal aspects of personality you're curious about. Stay open to variations in tone as well, such as going from serious to comic. Checking out your hero's mettle in a skyjacking may be useful, but what does he do about an infant with diarrhea when there are no clean diapers in the house? I would particularly urge people writing comedies to put their characters into serious disaster situations—so much comedy lately is cartoonish because the characters are so implausible. This etude is a way of making your funny people real human beings.

Also, be very open to the concept of disaster. I've referred mostly to cataclysmic events so far, but a disaster could be a failing grade or a bad hair day. It's all in the mind, age, maturity, and value scale of the person.

A twist would be to explore unexpected events that are the opposite of disasters but perhaps equally daunting such as surprise parties or winning a lottery. Again, the purpose is to test the parameters of your characters' personalities.

Lastly, don't ignore the possibility of this disaster not just being incorporated into your plot but even framing it. I'm thinking of the hurricane in *Key Largo*; the loss of Belle Reve, the family home, in *A Streetcar Named Desire*; or the sudden crash of the title character's marriage in *Edmond*. Disaster is the natural stuff of theatricality.

SEE ALSO: Being There Etudes, Entrances and Exits, Environmental Etude, Place Explorations, and Situation Exploration.

Entrances and Exits

This is a very basic etude for character exploration. It is something that most actors do innately and something you may have been doing in your writing without thinking about until now.

The Etude

Explore what a character is doing before he enters a scene and what he does when leaving. This etude is especially useful for a play you're about to work on, but will also help with a piece you've already finished and want to flesh out or reexplore. The depth to which you take this exercise is entirely up to you, but the purpose is to discover as openly as possible what your character's choices are in a given circumstance.

For example, I once played a character who was falling in love with a younger character. In one important scene my character finally knew that the other was returning his feelings. My director said, what do you do after this scene? I said I didn't know. She said, let's improvise. So I bid goodnight to the other character, exited the playing area, and discovered that I was walking on the beach—which was quite logical, since the setting was a beach house. As I took in the imaginary beach and ocean in the moonlight, I felt an exhilaration come over me that I couldn't contain, so I took my shoes off and started running. I ran down the beach until I was out of breath, then stopped and let the waves lap on my feet and bury them in wet sand while I stared out at the sea. Man, was I in love.

After that experience, every time we played that scene, I could start my exit knowing I wanted to go onto the beach. Besides filling out the character's world, this knowledge gave me an exit that was more than just leaving the stage. My character didn't know he wanted to run on the beach yet, but he knew he didn't want to go right home, and the beach was right there. This is a crucial working concept for an actor because it prevents him from "dropping the scene" on the way out and encourages that actor to carry the life of the scene and the character all the way through.

Your work in this etude can and should include creating the outside environments as well. What is the neighborhood like, how do the characters get to this place, what do they see along the way, is there a busy highway just outside the window?

Variations

Discover if any characters in the play cross paths offstage and what those scenes could contribute to the play onstage. If any of them are in cahoots, you will also want to explore the scenes not included in the play where they are plotting and scheming.

SEE ALSO: Behavior to Inevitable Words, Being There Etudes, Comings And Goings, Disaster, Extreme Mood, Place Explorations, and Subplot.

Extreme Mood

My view of theatre is that every moment should be as emotionally charged as possible. This means playing things dramatically and going after your objective 100 percent so that each moment is both interesting to watch and palpable to the audience. The bottom line is that theatre is not life; it's theatrical.

The work of the playwright should always be emotionally charged as well. This means high stakes, strong characterizations, and potent dialogue. Unfortunately, a good deal of the work I read is conversation masquerading as dialogue, and the resultant characters are about as exciting as dishwater. This etude is designed to help you keep your dialogue and your characters out of the mundane and move them into the dramatic.

The Etude

Rewrite a scene that now seems flat to you emotionally by pushing the scene to its emotional peak. Make sure each character feels that his need is at the level of life or death, even if that makes the behavior absurd. Give your characters a full emotional exploration and force each character to struggle for his objective as actively as possible. Certainly avoid letting any character be passive.

The end result of this probably won't be a usable rewrite of the scene in question—the display will very likely be too extreme—but you will see whether the original stakes and feelings were high enough. In the postanalysis process, ask yourself questions comparing the original characterization and what emerges from this etude. What you discover from the comparison should disclose more depth in the character, and should in turn provide stronger objectives and dialogue. A character whose objectives are very heated will tend to speak more heatedly than a character who is aimlessly wandering through a play with halfhearted needs.

In both the process of doing this exercise and in the post-analysis, keep a vigilant eye on the dialogue. Is the speech muscular or just chitchat? If you're really pushing your characters to their emotional extremes, they can't remain conversational. You may need to rethink your ideas of dialogue. Perhaps you need to change your style and approach, or perhaps your style and approach just don't apply to highly charged theatre, which is perfectly fine. Your choices should always be informed.

Variations

Have only one character in the scene set at an extreme mood to see where this takes the scene; do the same with each of the other characters in turn.

SEE ALSO: Disaster, Emotional Winds, Film Game, Imperatives Only, and Word Choice.

Free Time

This exercise looks at how a character spends free time and how that effort informs his personality. I remember being really amazed when a friend who seemed rather rigid physically and unathletic made a series of phenomenal dives at a swimming pool. "Oh, I competed in college," he said, like it was nothing. This led me to take a closer look at what people do in the way of hobbies and sports, because they often reveal otherwise hidden abilities and interests. This etude is related to three that follow (Other Attribute, Personal Quality, and What Do I Do for a Living), but differs because it is exclusively based on exploring a character's choice of how to fill free time.

The Etude

Decide on the structure of your character's daily life: get up at six, work at the library from nine to noon, take one-hour lunch, go back to work from one to five, and eat at home. Then what? Consider what this person does with his free time. Does the character play racquetball on his lunch hour? Does the character dress up like Sherlock Holmes for mystery parties at night? Does he like bingo or reading Dickens? Is he a couch potato? If so, what does he like to watch? I know a person who has three videotape recorders to tape dozens of shows each week because he really likes to study TV as a form. What if your character is somebody who has virtually no free time because he works, has kids, and takes care of the home with his spouse? What might he do with the half-hour per day he can claim as his own?

SEE ALSO: Age Explorations, Being There Etudes, Best Friend, Familiarity Etude, Other Attribute, Personal Quality, Place Explorations, Secret Behavior, Status Etude, What Do I Do for a Living?, and Word Choice.

Imperatives Only

This etude offers an alternative to the Questions Only etude below. The Questions Only etude examines evasion and denial, and Imperatives Only looks at control, power, and the attitude behind the desire to control.

The Etude

Write or rewrite a scene in which the characters are limited to making imperative statements to (or at) each other. The imperative form is used for giving commands or expressing the will to influence another's behavior: "Pick up that trash, walk to the wastebasket, drop it in," or, "You really must do something about your weight."

Obvious choices here might be a domineering parent manipulating a child or a boss browbeating an employee, but you can go much deeper if one ground rule is followed carefully: make both characters active. If you limit your exploration to one active and one passive character, then all you will discover is how character A controls character B. However, if you make both characters strong and actively in pursuit of meaningful objectives, the dynamic of the exploration becomes far more complex and challenging.

Rewriting an existing scene is a particularly useful way of taking a look at a character who may be passive. By forcing this character to use the imperative and be assertive, you can discover a stronger side—maybe even liberating a weakish character to play a more vital role in your play. You needn't worry about incorporating the etude back into the play, but you should make a clear choice of why this character is being assertive now (i.e., she's drunk and she's been fired and no longer cares) so that the shift in the character's behavior is organic.

This etude also offers a very interesting way to explore and develop characters because it shows very quickly what perceptions A and B have about each other simply by showing what they think they can command the other to do. In turn, you can see the vulnerabilities in the characters. Lastly, whether exploring an existing character or a potential one, the etude is a hands-on reminder to give each character strong objectives. If you haven't already tried Extreme Mood, the previous etude, you should. There are definite correlations between these two exercises.

This etude is likely to force an argument between the two characters—people bridle at being told what to do. And an argument may be a way for you to make an inactive scene more vital and energized. Certainly you will find out quickly how your characters react, where they're defensive, how they fight, and so on.

Variations

Make a strong, active character intentionally passive: put this person in a situation in which he no longer has his normal power or status. What happens? Another option is to make both characters in a scene passive, which puts them into a situation in which neither wants control. This approach suggests many comic possibilities.

SEE ALSO: Best Friend, Character Collaboration, Dialogue Collaboration, Emotional Winds, Extreme Mood, Questions Only, Status Etude, and Word Choice.

Normal Day

A "normal" day is what a character or group of characters has going before a play starts. In a sense, all plays are about time periods when things are out of joint. Studying what your character would consider a normal day, you can better understand and exploit the contrasts brought on when things are thrown out of kilter. This etude will also probably reveal what a character is often trying to accomplish in a play—getting back to the normalcy that existed before or creating a new normalcy.

This drive is suggestive because sometimes the character's notion of what was normal is skewed or completely distorted. Look at Sam Shepard's *Fool for Love*, which has as one of its main conflicts a battle over perceptions and memories of what was normal (or real) before the time of the play. Keep in mind that we all tend to repaint the past in colors we like, so your study of a character's idea of normal might be a study in lies, denial, and fantasies, as with Blanche DuBois in A *Streetcar Named Desire*.

The Etude

Construct a normal, typical day for a character you want to explore. You might start with a kind of itinerary: he wakes up at 6:00, stumbles into the bathroom, emerges at 6:15, goes to the kitchen where the coffee pot needs to be cleaned, and so on. Be as detailed as you can because each specific will take you deeper into the psyche of the character. Include information about the character's living space, job, friends, and so on (which is why you should do the other etudes first).

The next step is to write some scenes of this normal day. Find your character's voice and demeanor while focused on routine but theatrically interesting events. Good choices are times of the day when the character is having the most fun or feeling the most stressed; pick times that have dramatic qualities to them and will be fun to write. As with all of these etudes, stay open to surprises and don't manipulate the character's life; try to treat this exercise as if you're documenting a real life.

Variations

Play with the difference between a normal work day and a normal weekend day; introduce a variety of characters into the day who have various impacts on your character (a bill collector, a childhood sweetheart, or the mother-in-law); or combine the etude with others that complicate the normal day (such as Disaster). This is your character to explore, so it's up to you to determine what you want to know and discover and how many angles you wish to look at this character from.

Finally, avoid using your normal day exploration as the basis for a play that hinges on a what-happened-in-the-past kind of plot. Such structures are often very passive stories because they're about versions of something we don't see ourselves. If you insist, read some plays dealing with this kind of story basis and that employ unusual and challenging structures. Some of the best examples include *The Model Apartment, Fool for Love,* and *Rashomon.*

SEE ALSO: Age Explorations, Best Friend, Change of Time, Disaster, Free Time, Place Explorations, Status Etude, What Do I Do for a Living?, and Where Do I Live?

Other Attribute

The basis for this exercise is seeking out the opposite qualities of a character as written. In other words: look for the good in a villain or for the flaws in a hero. The underlying concept here is the recognition that all people like or dislike some things about themselves and therefore may be vain or insecure at some unrevealed level. A villain thinks he's right and acts on that belief; a hero does the same. Since there's not much difference between the two except on the moral scale, actors need to explore the other possibilities in that character's personality to avoid clichés. This technique will help you discover (or create) the hidden places in which a character may be vulnerable or blindly egocentric.

The Etude

Select a character you want to explore and put that character in a situation with a chance to behave differently than the character does in the play. I use the word *chance* here because it's not so important to show a villain being good as it is to explore a situation in which the character has the option to do good. Your effort will be to discover why that person chooses as he did at a given moment. For instance, if your villain never even considered the option to do good, you have a character who is off the normal scale—a Hannibal Lektor—and that's vital to know. With a situation like this you might want to incorporate aspects of the Age Exploration etudes so you can find your way back to a time when the character became socio- or psychopathic.

It's important here as always to keep our terms relative. Not all characters are villains or heroes of course, so one point of this exercise is to find those other, additional qualities about your characters that will flesh them out further for your play. And these qualities do not have to be based in moral issues. I remember the meanest, loudest sergeant we had in basic training saying, "Just go back to sleep, son," in this really gentle voice when he inadvertently woke me while doing one of those sneaky 3:00 A.M. inspections. I never saw that quality of kindness in him at any other time, but I never forgot it, either. The central issues are the discovery of qualities in your characters you might not have expected and the use of those discoveries to broaden the personality of those characters.

Variations

Explore the time when a character did act in the opposite way from how we see him in the play. You might find it quite challenging to write a villain being a really good person or vice versa. Another alternative would be to examine characters through their conscience about a decision. Brian Friel did this literally in *Philadelphia, Here I Come* when he put the main character's alter ego on stage with the character; and Eugene O'Neill did this and more in *Strange Interlude*, when the characters spoke their true private thoughts along with their public utterances (see the Spoken Subtext etude below for more on this).

SEE ALSO: Age Explorations, Best Friend, Character Collaboration, Extreme Mood, Emotional Winds, Familiarity Etude, Problem-Solving Monologue, Secret Past, Situation Exploration, and Spoken Subtext.

Personal Quality

One of the things I find interesting about people is vanity, even if they lack it. So many of us have such skewed or inflated visions of ourselves that I often wonder how (or if) we manage to meet any-body else in this world on honest terms. It seems to me that a great many of us have adapted functional personas that are publicly acceptable in lieu of letting our real selves out. Getting close to oth-ers means finding out about those really private aspects. This exer-cise is based on revealing these private vanities and anxieties.

The Etude

Write a scene in which a character is either inordinately proud or inordinately ashamed of a quality or inability. The primary intent is for you to consider a new character, but a variation below suggests an alternative. The scene should not be directly about the personal quality in question but should be affected by it. Some simple exam-ples would be a woman with a deep fear of gaining weight who tries to avoid cake and ice cream at her niece's birthday party; a man who is unusually vain about his muscles trying to cope with something that is just too heavy for him; and a super bright kid who has to hide his intelligence from other kids.

Variations

Explore a character who's in a play already. There are two ways of doing this. One is to follow the basic etude above and explore in public a private quality or ability. The other is to write a scene in which the character suddenly develops a personal quality he never had before: all at once he's 100 pounds heavier, twice as smart, or able to do slam dunks. The purpose is to examine a character who feels a bit lacking or overendowed in dimension.

For instance, in a recent workshop a playwright was told that his domineering father character was a cliché. The playwright was very defensive and resistant to this comment, and so very little was done to help the father's character. My suggestion to a more open writer would have been to try this etude to see what this father was vain about. Since music was an issue in the play, perhaps the father's per-sonal quality could have been that he was a wonderful dancer. Giving that character the chance to express this quality would have been a solid exploration for the playwright and perhaps would have answered some of the problems. In other words, the father's domination would have been based on a misguided sense of superiority with regard to music and therefore would have made him less a "typical" father. This etude and the others suggested below will provide a range of exploration for your characters and keep them from being superficial.

SEE ALSO: Age Explorations, Best Friend, Character Collaboration, Free Time, Neuroses, Other Attribute, Personal Problem, Secret Behavior, Secret Objective, and Status Etude.

Prop Etude

The point of this exercise is to explore the possibilities that a prop may create for a character. This gives you the opportunity to look at aspects of a character you might not normally consider.

The Etude

Select a character from an existing play and give that character scenes in which he has a prop to work with. You can simply introduce the prop into an existing scene but be aware that you must allow the prop to become expressive. You may choose a very simple prop like a handkerchief or something quite outrageous like a live lobster or an egg about to hatch. Keep in mind that the scene should not be about the prop. Rather, it should be that the use of the prop gives expression to the scene. If you're having trouble integrating the prop into an existing scene, then write an original scene with the same characters and this added prop. The main purpose here is not to rewrite the scene or play (although ideas may come from the etude) but to reconsider the character through this prop.

An additional focus is to look at how characters use their bodies, as well as what use they make of a prop. You may discover that your character can juggle and do sleight of hand, or you may find that your character is all thumbs. These discoveries may lead you to some very interesting possibilities for the characters later on, such as what kind of hand gestures they would use under stress or when they're happy.

Now, be aware that you might be poaching on the grounds of the actors and director with this exercise, so use it judiciously. I think it is vital for playwrights to craft their characters as wholly as possible, but you must leave room for the creative work of your collaborators. A well-trained and talented actor will more than like-ly find the kind of prop or gestures that will give full expression to your characters, and excellent directors will encourage their actors to do the same. This exercise is not necessarily intended for you to do their work for them, in other words. However, since it is extreme-ly useful for you to do this exercise to discover abilities and expres-siveness in your characters, you might leave the prop(s) as a sug-gestion rather than something set in concrete. For example, if your character is a very nervous person and you found that he's always playing with Greek "worry beads," then you can indicate that in the script. Be open, though, to the actor who plays this character for you because he may find ways of giving far greater expression to the ner-vousness by playing with his clothes, biting his nails, or by finding a totally unexpected prop.

SEE ALSO: Behavior to Inevitable Words, Character Collaboration, Normal Day, Secret Behavior, What I Do for a Living?, and Where Do I Live?

Questions Only

This etude presents you with a useful discipline for developing your technical skills with a stimulating character exploration.

The Etude

Write a scene between two characters in which they may only respond to each other with questions. You will automatically create a situa-tion in which neither character can get a direct answer. The lines must be legitimate questions rather than declarative or imperative state-ments with a questioning word or phrase tacked on (such as adding "don't you agree?" after a statement such as "You are a yutz"). You can use the exercise as a character study or you can rewrite a scene that needs more focus on states of denial or on an argument.

This exercise is a quick and effective way of creating or depicting a relationship in a state of tension. Part of the challenge for the writer is to see how long you can sustain the etude as a legitimate scene that keeps moving forward using only questions. You may find at first that you're working with random questions; however, in order to sustain the scene you will need to give each person a clear set of objectives that avoidance or argumentiveness helps attain. It doesn't matter if you start the scene randomly—you will find very quickly that either the objectives will reveal themselves or that the scene will go nowhere.

Another layer is to discover the character's need to deny or be argumentative. Some people are evasive because they prefer evasion, while others may avoid a direct answer because they really have something to hide. Still others may be exceptionally shy, introverted, or traumatized. The same may be true for people who argue all the time. Your postanalysis of the exercise should include consideration of this need aspect, but you should also give some thought to the nature of the word choices and the kinds of questions the characters ask to get another angle on the personalities.

You can also use the exercise to discover the problem between two characters. If the evasion on both sides is really strong, the etude can reveal what's at stake by making clear what is being avoided. You can also reveal the nature of the evasion or argument in the sense that it may be the whole basis for the relationship. Some people just like to fight.

This exercise can also be used as a way of starting a scene in a play when you have no idea how to get going. I recommend this etude in particular because it helps set up an argument so immediately and gives you such a fun dynamic to play with.

Variations

Have one character repeat what the other says as a torment; or simply not answer a series of questions put out by the other; or have one character only answering yes, no, or the shortest response possible to a series of questions. You might also give each character opposing moods or motives for the questions.

SEE ALSO: Behavior to Inevitable Words, Best Friend, Character Collaboration, Dialogue Collaboration, Familiarity Etude, Imperatives Only, Secret Objective, Status Etude, Vocal Distinctions, and Word Choice.

Secret Past

This is a variation on the etudes Secret Objective and Secret Behavior in the chapter on technique. This exercise differs by dealing with something from a character's history now having a direct effect on the present. In the other two etudes, the secrets are about something a character secretly wants or about behavior the character is trying to keep private. The essence of Secret Past is shown in Arthur Miller's *All My Sons* when Joe Kelleher tries to keep his past destructive choices hidden from view, but everything keeps bringing that past back to life. A different example is *Getting Out* by Marsha Norman. Here, a character's past and present selves war with each other. There are many additional plays that use this essential concept.

The Etude

Write an original scene in which a character's past is catching up to him. This past could be something very dark and terrible or something silly (he once dressed as a female on a bet). It could even be something good that the character now has moved away from (she was once a champion tennis player but now wants to be accepted as a doctor). The point is to allow this past to affect the character's present. Remember that you have the option of letting the past secret be revealed to the other character(s). In fact, it's a fun edge to play with letting them almost find out, just to see what that does to your primary character.

Use this etude to examine a new character or to play with one in an existing script. The exploration may not show up in the plot of the play but will provide you with depth in the characterization.

Variations

Write a scene or scenes in which the secret comes to light. This puts this etude in combination with the key etude version of the Age Explorations. A slightly different approach would be to write the key event of the secret past and match it up with a similar key event in the present.

Another twist on the basic etude would be to give the other character in the scene a secret as well—perhaps even a related secret. Imagine if two members of some religious order recognized each other as torturer and victim from another time or as former lovers. You could also extend this etude by examining your character through a series of different past secrets.

SEE ALSO: Age Explorations, Familiarity Etude, Secret Behavior, and Secret Objective.

Spoken Subtext

Sometimes a character eludes us because we don't know what that character wants or feels. This etude is a very direct way at getting at what's going on inside the character. Subtext is the meaning between the lines and affects how a given line of text will be said. If you ask three people how they are, and if one is depressed, the next bubbly, and the third quite angry, the answer of "Fine" will have three very different meanings. Similarly, subtext expresses unspoken ambition or need, so that a "Hi!" at the water cooler at 2:00 P.M. is quite different from a "Hi!" at a bar at 2 A.M.

Spoken Subtext is an exercise I've used quite a bit with actors because it helps me to gauge immediately how connected they are to their characters. By asking an actor to speak out the subtext, you can discover that he believes his character is a "little nervous" when the character is actually completely terrorized. In this sense, spoken subtext also has a great deal to do with the degree of what's beneath the lines.

The Etude

Write a scene in which the characters speak out their subtext in combination with their lines—whether before or interspersed between portions of a line. Employ either a previously written character or a new one.

By way of example, if our character says "Hi!" in a bar at 2:00 A.M., the subtext might go like this:

Ed: |Oh, man, it's almost two and I haven't met anybody yet that wasn't weird. If I have to go home by myself again tonight, I'm going to—hey, wait a second, look at this woman in that back booth, I never noticed her before. And, hold everything, she's reading a book, what is she reading, please let it be something worth—yes! William Kennedy, we've discovered intelligent life here!|
|He approaches the woman's table|
Hi!

Now, this subtext may show you a variety of things. Let's assume what previously existed was the stage direction and "Hi!" The exercise may show you that you haven't done enough work prior to that line to show the condition Ed was in—the spoken subtext reveals things previously unknown. On the other hand, it may show that you hadn't considered the degree of Ed's condition, even though you may have planted enough behavior to convey his general state of mind. Or it may reveal to you something previously unforeseen or unconsidered—it surprised me when I wrote in the sample that Ed likes William Kennedy. This could lead me to have Ed and the woman in the booth discuss Kennedy's work as a way of revealing aspects of their personalities.

I could also have Ed and the woman, Alice, continue their dialogue with subtext:

Ed: Hi! |Oh, brother, what a brilliant opening line.|
Alice: Hi. |Gee, hope that didn't sound too eager or, worse, maybe a little brittle. Oh, dear, he's got nice eyes—watch out.|

This etude lets you examine the characters' reactions to themselves and to each other, which can be extremely helpful in discovering motivation, relationship, the level of familiarity in the dialogue, and so forth. Certainly you'd want to consider your word choice for the scene. "Well, hello there!" might be more evocative than "Hi." Another possibility altogether is that you might end up incorporating some of the subtext into the dialogue just to open up the scene a little or to give it a different flavor. For example, I thought it would be funny if she were reading Mickey Spillane and they talked to each other in Spillaneish:

Ed: The night was sultry, and so was she. Hi.
Alice: She'd seen better, maybe, but not this year. Hi yourself. Pull up a chair.

You can go on from here ad infinitum (or ad nauseam). The main thing is to have a great time letting those normally private thoughts get expressed and to allow this process to thoroughly roam around the characters' feelings, needs, and wants.

Variations
Decide whether the characters hear each other's subtext. If we went back to the first Ed and Alice exchange, we might unbracket everything subtextual and make it understood that they do hear each

other's subtexts—what would happen then? What if only one could hear and not the other? What if both characters had the same subtext, or if their subtexts were diametrically opposed. If you're really having a rough road with a scene, you should try all of these variations to try to find out what's going on—or what could be going on—with your characters.

SEE ALSO: Other Attribute, Personal Problem, Personal Quality, Problem-Solving Monologue, Secret Behavior, Secret Objective, and Secret Past.

Status Etude

Keith Johnstone's book *Impro: Improvisation and the Theatre* (Theatre Arts Books; Routledge, Chapman and Hall; New York) contains lots of terrific exercises for actors and makes many stimulating and challenging observations about ways of thinking about theatre. I recommend the book highly if you're not already familiar with it.

One of Johnstone's key concepts is status. Status can mean your character has (or believes he has) more money, a better job, or is smarter, stronger, and so on, or that he has less and is worse. This awareness puts you on more or less than an equal footing so you know if your character is, for instance, trying to get up to another level or protecting the level he is on. Status keeps you from making assumptions about your character because you must check your status against that of every other character in the play and then deal with your status. Johnstone suggests that the status difference exploration go just a little above or below the true place of the character, but my suggestion is that you range across a broader set of possibilities.

I particularly responded to Johnstone's concept in terms of a character's private assessment of his state or condition as compared to the other character(s) in the scene. In other words, if I'm playing Polonius I would have to admit that I might never have as much royal swat as Hamlet, Gertrude, or Claudius, but I could certainly believe I'm smarter than all of them. When I confront Hamlet alone, I could certainly believe my advanced years and wisdom would make me more capable of dealing with his "affliction," and when he confounds me in that confrontation, I can avoid looking foolish by being angry at him for his lack of respect for my senior age and wisdom. As

Polonius, I must believe I have a really superior status—it helps explain his motivations and what makes him funny.

You can use status to reexamine an existing play, which I would strongly recommend because it may reveal a whole world of levels you never thought about. Or you can explore characters you're interested in for a new play. You might also reread a variety of plays with this perspective in mind. Status is a factor in a great many plays but exists on a variety of planes. David Mamet's *Glengarry Glen Ross*, for example, is based strongly on the forced shifting of status during the action of the play and how the characters respond to threats to their status. Marsha Norman's *'Night, Mother*, on the other hand, is based more subtly on the kind of status imposed in a closed society or protected environment—in this instance, a mother knowing things about her daughter that the daughter doesn't know but should.

I would also suggest taking a look around you for status. After reading Johnstone's book, I was astonished to see how many kinds of statuses exist. Status ranges from who is the coolest in the group to who's got the best Christmas lights on the block to who wears the winning team's logo. My first impression with Johnstone was that he was writing strictly from a British world view with all that class awareness, but after some reflection I discovered that America is absolutely riddled with status consciousness, particularly in the way we represent ourselves through our possessions or borrow our identities from the famous and successful.

The Etude

Write an exploration in which characters from an existing play or new characters in development are put into a context that calls their sense of status into play. Focus on one character's status at a time. You might write separate scenes in which Mark acts out his higher status in the office on Jim and then Jim destroys Mark on the basketball court. Of course, you should play with both characters' sense of status at the same time.

Variations

There are countless variations on this basic exercise, but keep in mind that status can mean a wide variety of things without necessarily being negative or competitive. A person of higher rank in an academic or religious community might never use that status to undermine the standing of another member, but the status differences will still exist in each character's awareness of the other. In fact, a basic and essential variation on this etude would be to place your main character in a wide range of status circumstances, choosing situations that will bring out an assortment of status reactions on the character's part.

It could be great fun to combine Status with any of the Age Explorations. What status means at the age of nine, eighteen, or seventy-two can be extremely different. This combination would give you a wide range of opportunities to get into the personality of your character. You could also combine status with something a little less obvious, like the Word Choice or Vocal Distinctions etudes, where status becomes more a matter of verbal expression. There are a number of other combinations below, but you should look for more as well.

A last suggestion would be to reread your own plays with an eye to status as a key factor. There may be concerns with status that you had no awareness of. In fact, any time you can go back to your earlier work with a new perspective you should, just to have the pleasure of surprising yourself. This suggestion would also apply to rereading various prior works after any completed etude to be able to say, "Hey, look at how well I used props there or status here." Technique and craftsmanship momentarily aside, there are times when ideas just spring out of us in a thoroughly muse-driven way we ought to allow ourselves to appreciate.

SEE ALSO: Age Explorations, Behavior to Inevitable Words, Best Friend, Familiarity Etude, Neuroses, Personal Quality, Secret Behavior, Secret Objective, Secret Past, Spoken Subtext, Vocal Distinctions, and Word Choice.

What Do I Do for a Living?

The focus of this etude is developing a character's work history. Your approach can be creative in part and research oriented in part. The research is particularly important because it can enable you to find all kinds of specifics and particulars about a character that would be wonderful as personality elements in a script. Imagine a character who walks with a perpetual stoop because he was a miner, a character who is almost hawklike with his eyes because he was a fire spotter, or a woman who is extremely precise with her hands because she is a brain surgeon. Even relatively nondescript jobs have peculiarities. I knew an accountant who had a constant squint, permanent ink stains on his fingers and a huge writer's bump on one finger. He also had the ability to audit a restaurant check in record time and divide it up for individual payments, tax and tip included.

Jobs also reflect our outlook on life. An actor friend is constantly worried about money because his life is typically limited by uncertain employment. Another friend was a teenage car fanatic and always underneath somebody's rebuilt Ford or Chevy. He lost a leg in Vietnam, got a Ph.D. in special education, and has a very profitable side business in restoring antique cars. He may not be able to get under the cars himself so easily any more but his passion remains. Even becoming a parent is emphatically its own kind of job and changes one's perspective on the whole world.

The Etude

Choosing any character, write about how that character's job affects behavior, physical expression, language, and so on. This exercise is multileveled and designed to give you a wide range of observations about this character in relation to what he does for a living. The levels should be considered in the sequence detailed below.

The first is to research the job you've selected for this character. Most people are very flattered when you want to know about their jobs and glad to have you come observe. What you would learn from a first-hand visit to see steelmaking, or to watch paramedics in action is almost beyond valuation. If it's not possible to be in the actual site, then interviewing people is an excellent alternative. You might want to look for your chosen job in Studs Terkel's phenomenal book *Working* to have a starting point and then try some interviews on your own.

If you're unable to find a way to visit a job or interview, there are certainly a multitude of information sources available. Consider both library research as well as direct source research, such as going to a computer company for information on what a computer programmer does or visiting a trade school or university that trains programmers.

The second level of this etude is to create the workplace for your character and write a scene set in this place. You may discover not only a thousand details of what he does but more knowledge of who he is; such an exploration is related to the Status etude above. I'd been to visit my father's workplace but I never fully saw him until I worked in the steel mill myself for a couple of summers. Then I could easily notice the pride in his walk, the certainty of his actions and voice, and the respect shown to him by the people who worked with and for him. Until that point he'd just been my dad; afterwards, he became more of a somebody. I also began to recognize certain features about him at home—his exhaustion, stress, and sense of being besieged by phone calls from work.

Which leads us to placing your character in a nonjob situation while trying to retain as many of the job qualities possible in behavior, actions, and demeanor. Try to avoid the obvious and cheap-joke kind of choices like having a dentist putting his fingers in people's mouths at a party. Instead, look for ways in which the job affects your character's world view and sense of status. Our dentist, for instance, would be highly aware of people's teeth but in a quick, casual way. On the other hand, our dentist might have a keen interest in high-tech equipment because he uses it in his office or even a real passion for ceramics and pottery related to materials from his job. I must stress here that doing the first level of this etude is extremely important. You can, of course, make up all kinds of things for your character, but basing them on a real-life corollary would be much more alive and detailed.

If you chose to put your character in a social context at this level, for the third level put him in a more personal context. How would a guy who operates a jackhammer all day deal with eating if his hands shake? How would a lawyer who is trying a case involving severe food poisoning cope with making her meal that night or eating her husband's cooking? How would a dentist make love? Would the event be hygiene-obsessed?

Once you've had a chance to explore these levels, you should look for other levels on your own. These could include putting your character at a conference devoted to his job or having your character be a witness in a trial related to his work. You will have a great deal of behavior and viewpoint background to integrate into the play for this character or you may have an entirely new play that grows out of the world you've uncovered.

Lastly, you should use your own background of job(s) for this etude. If I know what it's like to sell shoes, work in a steel mill, pump gas, wait tables, be a librarian, and run a music rehearsal studio—just to name a few past jobs—I can apply those experiences to my characters and plays.

Variations

Try combining this etude with the Age Exploration etudes (and others listed below). There's certainly a difference between the guy who works in construction at twenty and the same guy who's still doing it at fifty. You can discover the nature of your characters through what they do for a living—whether it's a profession or a job, something they hate or love—and you can apply that nature into the world of the play. Be careful not to control the outcome. For example, if you have a character who is very quiet and who is a mail clerk in a large corporation, let him take a spin in the Disaster etude. If your character is a fearless firefighter, then Disaster is sort of redundant. You might need to go to something like Secret Behavior to discover that your firefighter really wants to sing a duet with Pavarotti. Avoid the obvious and use the etudes to allow the possibility of surprise and discovery.

SEE ALSO: Age Explorations, Disaster, Environmental Etude, Familiarity Etude, Normal Day, Problem-Solving Monologue, Secret Behavior, Secret Objective, Stage Directions Only, Vocal Distinctions, Where Do I Live?, and Word Choice.

Where Do I Live?

The purpose of this etude is to develop the world a character occupies outside of the setting of the play. It is the kind of exploration that an actor playing your character should do of course, but the purpose here is for you to deepen your own knowledge and awareness of the character. Your exploration need not appear in the play, but the texture provided by it will inform the play through richer characterizations.

The Etude

First, design the living space of your character with a basic ground plan. You should do a drawing, painting, or model of the space and make detailed decisions about the furniture, wall colors, and decorations.

Next, give your character a scene in which to occupy that space. The scene may be related to the play in the sense that it forms a foundation for your character's entrance or it may just be a scene that appeals to you as having potential to reveal the character vividly. This scene might be drawn from using a combination of other etudes like Free Time, Secret Behavior, or Secret Objective. What's crucial is the character's behavior in his own living space—how he relates to it, what it gives him the liberty to be or do, and how it may affect him differently from the setting of the play.

Variations

Combining this living space with the Disaster etude would be revealing. Suppose the character hated his apartment and it was accidently trashed by a wrecking ball—how would he feel about the apartment then?

Another basic variation would be to examine the character's reactions to other people living in his space. This sort of suggests *The Odd Couple*, but I hope you wouldn't leave it there. An extension would be someone just using part of the space, perhaps renting it during the character's work day as an office or studio.

This etude gives you so much to play with, I hope you'll explore it as fully as you can. What does the character like to eat at home? Does he cook, order out, or just microwave? What kind of clothes does he wear in public and what does he wear at home? What kind of habits or quirks does he have that only come out at home? Does he screen phone calls on his answering machine or dive at the phone before it completes a full ring? What does he see from his windows? Who are his neighbors?

I'll close out this etude with a reprise of what I said at the beginning of the chapter: don't forget that the character's time in the play is a fraction of their life. The etudes in this chapter are designed to help you think of your characters as complex and complete human beings.

SEE ALSO: Being There Etudes, Disaster, Free Time, Ground Plan Collaboration, Normal Day, Place Explorations, Secret Behavior, Secret Objective, and Site-Specific.

6
CHAPTER

Plot Etudes

THE ETUDES IN THIS CHAPTER FOCUS ON THE PROCESS OF finding, refining, and redefining storylines. This chapter and Chapter 7 will be very useful for extending and playing with new ideas that you want to develop further and for reexploring existing plots that have either gone flat, haywire, or otherwise off the chart.

Separating plot from structure is crucial. The two are often linked together as if identical, but nothing could be further from the truth. Plot is what you wish to show an audience; structure is how you intend to show that plot. Why, for example, use a hoop of fire in the circus? Because the what of that act is simply someone or something jumping through the hoop. Whether the hoop's on fire or coated with cream cheese, that's all that's going on. But the how is the risk the fire creates and the threat it seems to pose. The act is still the same old hoop jumping, but our perception of it is vastly heightened by fire. In this analogy, structure is the equivalent of fire. Your choice of your play's composition will be directly related to how you wish to have the play encounter your audience and vice versa.

The hoops and fire metaphor is not meant to suggest that structure is just effect or affect, although it can be when poorly conceived. I'm making a case here for the separation of plot and structure at the most elementary level. In the heaps of plays I read each year, I find too many that attempt to rely on slick structural and stylistic choices to mask weak and ill-conceived plots. Film is even worse these days, relying on all manner of bells and whistles to attempt to cover up thoroughly incredible plot elements. Plot is just the basic story, and it must be coherent, no matter the subject or style, from start to finish. But structure is the point of telling the story and the method by which the artist goes after a world view and the audience's mind, values, gut reactions, heart, and so on.

If *Betrayal* were written in a forward-moving storyline, it would just be a fairly typical potboiler about infidelity. With the kind of complex structural choices Pinter makes, however, we get a play that brilliantly examines the nature of betrayal, fidelity, love, angst, and so on, and also reveals the nature of the characters and of the era in which they lived.

The plot of your play is a segment of many other things. Your first job is to understand the nature of that segment in terms of the story it tells: born, suffered, and died; met, fell in love, and drifted apart. This story is naturally connected with the people whose story you're telling, so character enters immediately as well. There are many ways of figuring out plot—writing a treatment, doing an outline, putting scenes on notecards, but the etudes in this chapter are designed to help you approach plot through the application of theatrical writing methods.

Some of the etudes are for finding plots if you are having a difficult time coming up with ideas, and some are for playing with a plot you already have to reexamine its possibilities. It's likely that plot ideas will have come to you already from other chapters, but the focus here is specifically about helping you discover stories or improve on those ideas.

KEY ETUDE
Photo
This is an exercise for creating plots that I got from David Mark Cohen, the head of the playwriting program at the University of Texas at Austin. The name of this etude really refers to any still image, including paintings, sculptures, or pictures of either, as well as illustrations, billboards, wall murals, postcards, and so on.

The Etude
Find a source of photos unfamiliar to you and let an image that you find particularly striking propel you into a plot. Select sources initially

that are highly suggestive—photos of people in situations that are dramatic already—such as *The Family of Man* collection, the news photos of Weegee, or the work of Diane Arbus just to name three radically different sources. Most libraries have books by photographers, and some even have separate picture collections. There are dozens of photo magazines available every month. Avoid "photo essay" books, since the temptation there will be toward a literal reaction.

The catch with this exercise, in fact, is to avoid a literal take on the photo. It may be that the picture shows two happy little boys holding up a fish they caught. Instead of creating a plot about these chipper lads, consider one about two somewhat childish detectives who've caught a dangerous criminal. It really doesn't matter where you go from the image itself, only that you trust and follow your intuition as faithfully as possible. In order for this exploration to pay off at its optimal potential you might want to try doing a series of photos—one a week, say—just to give yourself some range of experiences and choices. You'll probably want to store these etudes for future reference.

Once you've had a chance to explore sources that are relatively concrete, you might want to try working from photographers (or other visual artists) whose approach is more abstract. Ralph Eugene Meatyard, for instance, made a collection of very disturbing images of the normal world. Ralph Gibson often focuses on abstracting the real into some other place or consciousness. The works of Robert Mapplethorpe, Deborah Turberville, Helmut Newton, and Cindy Sherman take our assumptions about identity, gender, and sexuality into other realms. We haven't even touched on painters such as Cassatt, Dali, Picasso, Monet, or Hockney, or the multitude of other visual artists available to us through books, magazines, and the Internet.

This etude largely lends itself to discovering plots and ideas for original work, but it's possible that you could use it for an existing play that has lost its fizz. Try reading the play and then looking through as big a collection of images as you can gather. Now reread the play and keep an eye on your inner process to see what images jump up as you go along. It's possible you'll get nothing, but then as Fats Waller once said, "One never knows, do one?"

Another approach to this same problem would be to work more from a director's perspective, looking through a pile of images for those that reflect the play "accurately" in terms of creating visual cognates or resonators—things that help to reflect the play back to you perhaps a bit more clearly and that are not tied so literally to your plot as to the impressions that started the plot.

Variations
Find music that works with the image(s)—whether literally or not is your choice—and let that help complicate the image, extend it, or work against it. For example, using really harsh music against a tender photo of young love might give you a potent juxtaposition for a very different plot than what the image alone would've suggested. It's up to you how to add to or distort the image(s) you're working with; any manner of pushing yourself away from a customary approach is worth pursuing.

SEE ALSO: Adaptation Etudes, Adapting to the Stage Etudes, Being There Etudes, Composing to Music, Film Game, Film Reversal, Newspaper, Place Explorations, and Site-Specific.

OTHER ETUDES
Adapting to the Stage 1: Adapting from Prose
This etude is related to the Adaptation Etudes in Chapter 4, but here you are adapting from other forms rather than to other forms. More importantly, you're doing this etude specifically for the purpose of learning about plot and for developing plot ideas.

The Etude
Choose a short story, novella, or portion of a novel and adapt it for the stage. This is harder than it sounds, but what you'll learn will be extremely useful.

Use this etude to develop a stronger sense of plot through a close examination of how others craft plot in their medium. The main caveat is to choose an active story to adapt and to avoid stories that are entirely vested in the inner life of a character. Such translations are very difficult to bring to the stage. Try redoing the etudes in Chapter 4 relating to adaptation before moving into this particular exercise. You should also look at other prose-to-stage adaptations to get a sense of the choices involved.

The essential rules of adaptation will apply: you must be faithful to the spirit and essentials of the source (i.e., characters and plot), but you'll likely need to make some shifts—especially in structure—to make the material play on the stage. It's through these shifts that you will learn the most; the very fact of coming to realize that the structure of a short story won't pay off theatrically unless you alter it will help you to understand the original author's intentions much more deeply, as well as your own intentions and sense of plot and structure.

Remember that adaptation is not literal; it involves making the thing being adapted one's own while being true to the purpose of the original. You must be very clear on the choices made by the original writer, who could have, after all, written the piece as a play. You must analyze the story with great care in terms of the mechanics: what is said, what is not said, what transitions are used, when dialogue is used rather than narrative, and so on. Working with these initial choices and struggling to reinterpret them for the stage will provide you with a lot of new ways of evaluating and approaching plot and structure.

Variation
Try adapting a nonfiction work, which could be far more tricky but would also result in new perspectives on plot. See the Newspaper etude.

SEE ALSO: Adaptation Etudes, Adapting to the Stage Etudes, Film Game, Film Reversal, Newspaper, Oral History, Photo, and Style Copy.

Adapting to the Stage 2: Adapting from Fables
Fairy tales, fables, and allegories are perfect sources for plot ideas and exercises especially when extrapolated into adult contexts. Contemporary examples include the work of the San Francisco Mime Troupe, El Teatro Campesino, and plays such as Story Theatre and Into the Woods, to mention a few. This is not to advocate fable-based plots above any others, but to extol them as fun seeds for the writer's craft. These kinds of highly imaginative resources free the writer from many of the usual conventions about character and plot because the starting point is fantasy and a world in which values, attitudes, and morals are right on the surface. In addition, there are

more and more sources of folk tales available as interest in the cultures of the entire planet expands. Unfamiliar stories make excellent starting material because they often challenge us to come out of our normal "folk roots" and experience cultures in which the magical and the real exist side by side in everyday life.

The Etude

Find a source of fairy tales, folk tales, or fables that captures your imagination. You might begin with those of your own childhood and then expand ethnically, racially, and religiously. Keep in mind that you're looking for material that triggers images in you that could serve as sources for plots. Above all, don't be too literal about anything you discover as a source.

Once you have material that gets you going, the next step is to write at least a few scenes. Remember that you're using this as an exercise to stimulate ideas—the play you come up with might not be a towering new work of art, but the point is that you'll have explored plot differently from the way you usually do.

The nice thing about these adaptation etudes is that you can do them when there's nothing else going on. Perhaps you're having a dry spell or maybe you've just finished a big project and need some mental gymnastics before the next larger work can be undertaken. Whatever the situation, these etudes are ideal for inspiration and distraction.

Variation

Try an approach based on improvisational exercises for theatre and comedy in which a group of actors is given a well-known fable to tell, but each actor is given a specific style in which to do it, such as telling Little Red Riding Hood in the style of a soap opera, a low-budget biker movie, a science fiction film, and a pornographic film. The way to do this on your own is to write a list of styles on notecards, then pick a fable and draw from the styles cards to see which way to write. You can vary this exercise further by beginning in one style and drawing for another while writing the same fable. You could even combine this variation with the Emotional Winds etude in this chapter and let the cards dictate both style and mood in as many ways as you'd like.

SEE ALSO: Adaptation Etudes, Adapting to the Stage Etudes, Emotional Winds, Film Game, Film Reversal, Newspaper, Notecard Shuffle, Oral History, Photo, and Style Copy.

Adapting to the Stage 3: Adapting from TV or Film

This etude is part adaptation and part original work—it really depends on how you want to approach it.

The Etude

Take the cast of a popular TV show from any era you're familiar with and write a series of scenes using those characters. You can do this etude with the purpose of trying to write something honest and truthful that could have been a plot for this particular show, or you can take a more comedic tack and massively subvert the original intention and see where it takes you. The honest and truthful method might lead you to take the characters from *The Brady Bunch* and write an episode of that show as it might have been done for the actual series; the subversive approach would be to switch genders on the characters, make them all social outcasts, and set the show in a remote or outrageous location—the Bradys as bikers in the outback.

The same approach can be done with film but the main restriction to any choice is that you work with something that's extremely well known. There is also an etude called Film Reversal that covers territory similar to this exercise.

The point is to learn from these sources by copying and/or satirizing them, although there is a middle area between these two extremes that would be worthwhile exploring as well. By examining the structure of how another plot is told, you will discover aspects of plot that could be quite valuable (especially shows like M*A*S*H that often had multiple plots interwoven in a very short format); you may also discover storylines that may be of some use to you.

SEE ALSO: Adaptation Etudes, Adapting to the Stage Etudes, Film Game, Film Reversal, Newspaper, Oral History, Photo, and Style Copy.

Being There 1

This exercise has all kinds of potential and is similar to the Ground Plan Collaboration in Chapter 8. This particular version depends on your access to a space (either a theatre or an open area, such as a dorm lobby, warehouse corner, or spare room in your home) where you can play with the arrangement of physical objects. What you can gain from this etude is the recognition that there is no single approach to developing plot ideas. We can either impose our own restrictions or create our own freedoms in our processes.

The Etude

In the space you've selected, create a set with whatever is available: boxes, chairs, door frames, flats, or pieces of cardboard cut out or taped up to emulate objects. Materials that are imaginative rather than literal are probably preferable in this situation because the challenge is to create the feeling of a space rather than an actual locale. Don't focus your set on any particular play or even a half-conceived plot—don't plan, just spend some time playing house in a theatrical context. Trust your instincts and don't worry about this set as a design for an audience—put the furniture and walls as you like them without regard to sightlines or anything else except what feels dramatic and interesting to you.

Once you've set up the environment to your liking, sit with it for a while, move around in it, look at it from an outside perspective, and see what begins to develop in your mind. Perhaps you've recreated an old known space without realizing it, a space you've heard of, or a space you know nothing about. Let your instincts tell you what kind of story suggests itself to you in this place. If nothing arrives, dismantle the set and do another and see where that one leads.

Once you have a story idea, there are a variety of directions you can then take. One would be to go home and write some scenes, and then bring them back and act them out on your own or with actors. Another option would be to improvise on your own in this space and see how the story develops. A third would be to invite some actors to the space, give them a bare-bones outline and have them improvise to see what evolves. These various approaches may help you find a more complete plot or may show you that this plot isn't worth pursuing, but you'll have come at the effort from an angle that is unique and that may serve you with a fuller purpose at some future point.

Variation

Predesign a set on paper and then try out that design in a real space to understand the translation. Much can be learned from designing a set and then "theatricalizing" the realized set by eliminating as many nonessential items as possible. Do you really need walls, the framed painting on the wall, or the full entertainment center? How can you approach the space in the most evocative fashion? What can you learn from a theatricalization about your plot ideas?

Obviously, this etude has a lot in common with those concerning Collaboration in Chapter 8. It also has excellent applications for writer's block (see Chapter 9).

SEE ALSO: Being There 2, Environmental Etude, Ground Plan Collaboration, Obstacle Exercise 2, Place Explorations, Prop Etude, Site-Specific, and Where Do I Live?

Being There 2

The difference between this etude and the Being There 1 is that this exercise uses real spaces rather than created spaces. The etude has three variations: the first takes inspiration from real spaces that are used for commonplace activities, and the others are based on real spaces in which something of historical or personal significance has occurred.

The Etude

First variation: Go to a variety of spaces that intrigue you—a doctor's waiting room, a chapel, a museum, or a colorful restaurant. Spend enough time there to get a sense of how and why the space is organized. Try to understand the space on the basis of function. Next, make a concerted effort to allow your intuitive self to run free with the fantasies and images that the space provokes, allowing yourself plenty of room to alter the space for dramatic purposes. Keep notes in some form on these images as possible future seeds for plots or plot elements. You might also combine this with Oral History by interviewing people who normally occupy these spaces and/or people who only visit them occasionally.

Second variation: Go to places where you know particular events have occurred. This could include visiting historic sites

(Gettysburg, Deeley Plaza) or locales where more recent events have occurred (the scene of an accident or a courthouse where a famous trial just finished) or places where past and present intersect, such as the Vietnam Wall or the United Nations. The choices are up to you, of course, which means that you'll need to follow your gut instincts. The places you choose may be randomly based on what's within reach of your ability to travel, or they may be thematically linked, if that's of interest to you and possible. The essence of this exercise is to use the stimuli available from the external world and allowing those stimuli to lead you to either new ideas for plots or to new vantage points from which to consider plots.

Third variation: Visit spaces that have only significance to you on a personal level: the high school, burger joint, bar, or park. This is something we all do, of course, but rarely with the intent of looking for plot-triggers and stimuli. Remember when you do this variation that the viewpoint needs to be based on looking for material for dramatic plots, not just nostalgia and/or autobiographical material. Perhaps the hardest thing to keep in mind at times is that we need to combine "write what you know" with an active sense of keeping it metaphorical and imaginative rather than literal and documentary.

SEE ALSO: Being There 1, Environmental Etude, Ground Plan Collaboration, Obstacle Exercise 2, Oral History, Place Explorations, Prop Etude, Site-Specific, and Where Do I Live?

Change of Time

This etude will work best with an existing scene that is not satisfactory, but you could also do it on a purely experimental basis by writing a scene first and using this etude to vary the scene.

The Etude

Rewrite a scene for a completely different time of day to see what happens when the scene is shifted from, say, late afternoon to three in the morning. The impact on the scene should range from nominal to major. Some people sitting around drinking and talking about the meaning of it all probably won't be affected by a time change from day to very late at night, but a scene in which a couple are having a very heated argument would be affected, because the feelings we have are often enhanced or exacerbated by the time of day.

While this etude is partially for technique exploration, its primary application is to plot, if only as a kind of yardstick. If the change in time has no special impact on the scene, it may be that the scene is perfect as is, or, conversely, that the scene is in need of other exploration because it may be too general or undramatic.

Variations

Take a given scene and explore the reality of the characters and the plot throughout a twenty-four-hour period: how is the argument at 6:00 A.M. with the baby crying as opposed to 5:30 P.M. when everybody's hungry and there's no dinner? Or explore the nature of a given scene or relationship if the scene is occurring a week earlier or later, or in a different year, month, or decade. What might your characters know that's different in another time in their lives? This particular angle asks you to take a hard look at your plot in terms of why it must happen when it does: that year, month, day, hour. Not all plots have to be this specific, of course, but for those that are, this etude will allow you to expose those particulars for your own needs.

SEE ALSO: Age Explorations, Free Time, Normal Day, Sensory Etudes, and Site-Specific.

Comings and Goings

The title of this etude is from a play called Comings and Goings by Megan Terry that depends on exits and entrances as transformations from one state of being to another and one level of relating to another. It is a useful play to read with regard to this etude, and it's a fun play to know anyway.

The focus here is on training the writer to deal with multiple objectives. The etude also stresses dealing with a large cast situation as an additional complication. Both goals will not only extend the writer's ability to craft scenes but add to the storehouse of plot ideas as well. It will also provide a hands-on method of approaching the essentials of farce style, which is built on the impact of entrances and exits on a given comic premise (you should read Moliere's works if you haven't already). However, comedy is not the only application or historical basis for this etude. After all, Shakespeare's plays are built on the shift of time, space, and plot evolving from entrances and exits.

The Etude

Write a scene that has at least four characters in it. First decide on a place where people can come and go with relative ease, such as a waiting room or reception hall. While continuing to move the scene forward, keep your additional focus on finding reasons for each character to leave the scene. These reasons must be organic to the character and not just whimsical ("Oh, I must go see the pony trot by!"). You must also find reasons for each character to return to the scene and contribute to its forward progress. You must have each character leave and return at least once during the scene. You also have to decide whether or not the comings and goings affect the plot of the scene, but they're likely to anyway.

Variation

Utilize a trio of characters and put them in a space where coming and going is more difficult, as with a couple in a therapy session with a counselor. The exercise is finding ways to have them exit and enter that will emphatically have an impact on the scene. Once you've tried the basic etude and this variation, you may discover other ways of using the basic exercise—some of the suggestions below provide some very interesting combinations to help this exploration. Certainly when you're working on a play and feel a bit stuck, this etude may prove very useful as a way of playing with possibilities.

SEE ALSO: Behavior to Inevitable Words, Entrances and Exits, Familiarity Etude, Mystery Imposition, Personal Problem, Place Explorations, Plot Collaboration, Secret Behavior, Secret Objective, Site-Specific, Stage Directions Only, and Where Do I Live?

Dreams

This etude is an excellent source of plot ideas and a fun exercise for freeing up your normal sense of structure.

The Etude

Write a scene based on a dream you recall. Do your best to write the scene in the same sequence as the dream without regard to transitions or logic. Let the flow of the dream reveal itself to you; dreams are often as much about juxtapositions of images as they are about the images themselves—a statement that's equally true for theatre and film. Also, try to be as faithful to the mood of the dream as to the details. If it was a nightmare, for example, are you able to capture the stuff that scared you awake? This exercise is in many ways like a freewriting session in which you follow the seemingly random flow of thought except that you are trying to record something you've already thought and thought of largely in symbols. You'll also need to fight off desires to interpret as you go or to alter things that might seem too revealing or scary. Stay faithful to the dream at all times.

Dreams are wonderful studies for artists because they don't obey linear structure or thought. Plays that drag the most usually have ignored the possibility of free movement from scene to scene, largely because they rely too much on lengthy transitions and descriptions that explain things to the audience rather than engaging them dramatically. There's nothing wrong with linear structure or with transitions when they're really needed, but a lot can be learned about leaping from key point to key point by studying and recreating your dreams.

The real question is, which rhythm works best for which play? Does the play need a continuous structure, or would it best benefit from a contiguous and nonlinear form instead? For a wonderful example of the use of contiguity, read *The Conduct of Life* by Maria Irene Fornes and take a close look at the first four scenes that may or may not be happening in a linear time frame. You may find that this play (among others) has a dreamlike feeling to it, perhaps because the playwright wants to detach us from our day-to-day A-B-C mindset and set us loose in a world built on a C-F-A-D-B structure so that we are forced to reexamine our view of reality and our own lives. Another quite literal example of dream-based work can be found in James Lapine's play *Twelve Dreams*.

Regardless of how you use this etude, be careful not to worry about interpreting dreams at the outset. Save interpretation for later, and rely on the inspiration of the endlessly creative subconscious part of yourself.

Variations

Rewrite a portion of a play you're working on as a dream to see what this does to the plot and/or structure. Sometimes by really shaking up our approach to a given work, we can free our minds from overly rigid views of it. Another choice would be to use someone else's dream as a scene to see how close you can get to that person's experience. In effect, you're trying to achieve oral history, so recording a recollection of the dream would be helpful. You can also ask the person to tell you the dream more than once to allow you to listen more intently and to give the teller the chance to recall details thoroughly. If you can't find people to share their dreams, try making some up through a character or the character's best friend.

SEE ALSO: Best Friend, Fantasy Scenario, Freewriting, Journal, Oral History, and Sensory Etudes.

Emotional Winds

This etude is based on an improvisational technique in which a group of actors will be asked to keep a storyline continuous but change the emotions as dictated by a group leader or side coach. The challenge is for the actor to keep the story moving forward without allowing the new emotional state to change the plot, which is usually a familiar fable or fairy tale.

The difference in this exercise is that you must allow the change of emotions to change the plot because the whole exploration is on the impact of emotions on story. Your purpose in the exercise is to discover plot possibilities by following the shift of emotions and seeing what evolves.

The Etude

On notecards, write as many emotions as you can think of. Keep the emotions general—angry, lonely, frightened, jubilant—to give yourself room to work. Shuffle the cards and begin writing a scene at random. At some point draw one card from the deck and keep writing the scene but in that new emotion. Allow these emotional winds to blow your plot, the characters, and their relationships all over the map.

The outcome of your first effort with this may be a crazy quilt you can't do much with, but if you continue to play and really let your mind follow the etude without prethinking, new ideas for plots and new perspectives on plot and structure will begin to emerge. This etude also has obvious applications for technique and character development as well but keep a focus on plot at the forefront of your efforts.

Variation

A good twist would be similar to other etudes using notecards: choose a new card for each new page, or set a timer and select a new card on a regular, timed basis.

SEE ALSO: Change of Time, Comings and Goings, Composing to Music, Entrances and Exits, Notecard Shuffle, and Plot Collaboration.

Fantasy Scenario

I was working recently with a wonderful playwright named Clay Nichols, who was in residence at PlayWorks, a play development program I direct. Clay was having trouble with a character in his play O.T. because he didn't know what the stakes were for her—what could be lost or gained in the unfolding of the plot. I suggested that he needed to have a better idea of what she'd hoped to gain in the actions preceding the time of the play (she'd decided to move to Dallas to live with a man she'd fallen in love with in Chicago). We came up with the idea of writing scenes and monologues in which Elizabeth, the character, revealed her fantasy expectations at the time of her decision to make the move. It paid off very well because the next sequence of scenes greatly clarified Elizabeth to us and enriched the depth and texture of the plot.

After this experience, it occurred to me that there were other ways of using a character's fantasy scenario, all of which will strengthen the character and supply a more detailed and layered plot.

The Etude

First variation: Either prior to or while you are working on a play write a variety of scenes and/or monologues in which your character gives full expression to her fantasies about how things will turn out for a given choice. Such choices could include moving to a new town, marrying someone, blowing her savings on an exotic vacation, or even planning suicide. Let the character have plenty of opportunities to speak out these fantasies to a variety of other characters because we tend to alter our levels of openness and honesty based on who we're speaking with. Also, make sure to explore the fantasies openly without worrying about how they will fit into a given plot. Keep your work exploratory.

Once you've had the opportunity to do a full exploration of these fantasy scenarios, you can begin to see how they will affect the plot. As always, be flexible: the fantasies may change the plot you had in mind or they may not work for the plot at all.

Second variation: Explore the fantasy life of one or more characters you're interested in but have no plot for as yet. Everyone has a constant fantasy track running—daydreams about incredible success or failure, romance, revenge, and so on. Plugging into that track in characters will show you a great deal of what they're about as people and provide many potential plot ideas.

Third variation: Using one or more characters from a play in which the plot seems to be going nowhere, write about the characters' fantasies as to where the plot should go. Stay open to serendipity. If a minor character wants to stage a rebellion and take over the play, let her go for it. Allow another character to discuss why the play isn't worth finishing at all. Just don't lose your sense of humor or perspective.

A multitude of other variations can be found in combination with the etudes listed below: consider the differences in fantasies at different ages, the nature of fantasies based on a secret past, and so on. There are likely to be a range of related etudes you'll develop on your own. There are no limits as to where this kind of exploration can take you.

SEE ALSO: Age Explorations, Best Friend, Dreams, Emotional Winds, Free Time, Freewriting, Neuroses, Personal Quality, Problem-Solving Monologue, Secret Behavior, Secret Objective, Secret Past, and They're Talking About You.

Found Situations

This etude is based on eavesdropping, something we all do naturally, and which many writers do constantly. The purpose of this exercise is to tune in to the life around you, to develop plot ideas as well as a better ear for dialogue and speech mannerisms.

Since "finding" a situation can amount to spying, I'll make several caveats for the etude. First, your eavesdropping should be done openly. You shouldn't listen through walls, in other words, but don't listen too obviously either. Second, eavesdropping should never be done maliciously or to get the "dirt" on somebody. Third, you should never betray a confidence. Fourth, the ideas you get and the dialogue you recall should never be utilized verbatim in a script. Just be careful not to violate people's privacy.

There's another perspective here, as well: I will often tell people I'm just meeting that I'm a writer, especially if they seem intent on telling me their stories. I also warn them that I have occasionally incorporated the stories of friends into my plays. This is just my way of telling them that the process is sometimes utterly unconscious and that I may not know I've retold someone's anecdote in a play until they remind me. In several instances, I've set out purposefully to fictionalize someone's story (a friend of mine was James Dean's girlfriend for a time, and who could pass that up?). Then I've gone to that person and asked for permission, shown them drafts of the play, and so on to avoid any hurt feelings or law suits.

The Etude

The objective of this exercise is to observe a situation and mentally record it for possible use later on. Writing down what was said at the time is a good way to keep a record and sharpen your sense of dialogue. There are several other points to the etude. One is to use these records as possible plot catalysts. Another is to use them as plot "texturizers," drawing on detail and nuances to help layer a story you're working on.

Once you're comfortable with your ability to listen and record with accuracy, you could take the etude into a more expressive place by creating a scene of your own based on the found situation. Try incorporating the actual words overheard into the scene or by just letting the situation be a stimulus. This particular exploration allows you to write a character based on the conscious observation of a real situation and then see what your further reactions are to the situation. In other words, you can examine your subjectivity and objectivity at the same time. Doing this aspect of the exercise on a regular basis will provide you with an array of plot choices for future use. In fact, it would probably be useful to keep a specific journal of found situations as a kind of incubator for future possibilities.

SEE ALSO: Age Explorations, Behavior to Inevitable Words, Being There, Best Friend, Dialogue Collaboration, Familiarity Etude, Oral History, Secret Behavior, Secret Objective, Secret Past, Site-Specific, Vocal Distinctions, and Word Choice.

Freewriting

Generally, the term freewriting applies to free association and the stream-of-consciousness jam session in which the writer tries to just follow thoughts on a page without regard to form or logic. The word is also applied sometimes to the creation of lists of ideas/thoughts for future use. This etude falls into the first category.

The Etude

Starting from any stimulus that appeals to you—a piece of music, a photo, a painting, a provocative sentence, a mental image—begin writing a scene without regard to its direction, form, import, adherence to the rules of basic playwriting, or anything else. Just write and keep writing until you get too tired to continue. Do not censor yourself or question a choice. Your ambition here is not coherence.

When you're done, put the piece away and do something for a time that will put your mind in a different place for an hour or a week. Once you've had this break, come back and look at your work and see where it went. Try to get a sense of what your mental progression was and what reactions you had to the stimulus. Your next step is the most important: try to get a sense of what the piece is about for you. Does it ramble incoherently? What is the essence of its story?

Freewriting is a very useful technique for all writers, of course. As a plot tool for a playwright it is aimed at freeing you from the usual choices, ideas, and approaches. Our nature as writers is to turn virtually everything we see into a story; freewriting is a method of getting at the stories lodged in our unconscious minds.

I won't belabor methods and variations. You are likely to discover far more than I could invent. Keep in mind there's no "wrong" or "right" way to freewrite so long as you let go of results, censorship, and logic and just let yourself write.

As always, combining this etude with others listed below can lead to some highly intriguing explorations.

SEE ALSO: Composing to Music, Dialogue Collaboration, Dreams, Emotional Winds, Fantasy Scenario, Found Situations, Newspaper, Notecard Shuffle, Photo, Prop Etude, and Writing Lyrics.

Get-in-Late/Get-out-Early

This etude challenges your plot's theatricality.

The Etude

The basic exercise is to start a scene as late in the action as you possibly can rather than provide the audience with the kind of slow build up that typically establishes place, time, ambiance, relationships, exposition, and so on in a linear, naturalistic pattern. You can write a scene specifically for the etude or apply it to a scene that is already written. In the case of the latter, your job is to hack as much from the front end of the scene as you can until you get to the hottest action you can without completely bewildering an audience.

Now, not all plays are about hot action per se, but let's not be too literal about definitions here. *Hamlet* begins late: a soldier is nervously standing guard when somebody shows up and scares him half out of his wits and we find that the castle's ramparts are haunted. We pick up the back story and some other details as we go further on, but we've started from nervous, scared, and haunted—pretty hot. *The Tempest* begins aboard a ship in the full fury of a storm at sea. Even *Oedipus Rex* begins with the town already in a state of terrible suffering and people crying to the king for help. The point is that most theatre works best when we are thrown into the midst of chaos and crisis; the audience is engaged dramatically right from the get-go.

In fact, my contention is that all plays are essentially detective stories: who's the ghost, what's he want, and what'll Hamlet do now that the ghost has told him the truth? And *Oedipus*, of course, is the original detective story with the original twist: finding the killer is finding yourself. The "explicit" detective story model is where the open dramatic question is the story. Along the way we get filled in on the who, how, where, when, and why, but our start and finish is based firmly on the what.

The get-out-early aspect doesn't necessarily refer just to the end of the play, but to the end of scenes so the playwright can take the greatest advantage of juxtaposition. If we see a young woman going crazy over two guys—a dashing young painter or a handsome athlete—and we leave the scene before knowing the choice, our curiosities are piqued to the maximum. And if in the next scene we arrive after the decision to find the young woman in a heated argument on the phone with her parents, all the while playing with some paintbrushes, then we know the answer to the prior scene's question even as we're being thrust forward into the next dramatic moment of the plot. And this is only one kind of juxtaposition. Others can involve symbolic gestures and meanings or philosophical matters. The absolute essence of the exercise is to keep the audience engaged, to propel it forward dramatically, and to do away with what it doesn't need to see.

Further, the etude encourages us to use the real tools of our craft. In his book On Directing Film (New York: Penguin Books), David Mamet talks about avoiding the kind of prosaic filmmaking that involves having the camera just trail along behind the main character. Instead, he advocates using cuts to link together crucial images and moments to tell a story through pure film language. This observation also applies to the stage and how we write for it.

If you read the masters—classics like Shakespeare, Sophocles, Chekov and moderns from O'Neill on through Shepard, Emily Mann, and Kushner—you will see that they all employ the techniques described in this etude. In fact, despite modern issues and certain contemporary devices, Angels in America is essentially constructed like a Shakespearean play. And I say, if it works, use it.

Of course, not every scene of every play can start late and end early, but there is much to be learned by using this etude as a method of developing scene-crafting skills and by letting it become a way of checking on scenes you've already written. How much of the scene do we absolutely need in order to understand it and to be engaged dramatically? Lastly, all plays need to have some kind of internal passion and drive, and this etude is a good way of discovering where the fire is.

Variation

Write a scene that begins and ends on one page only. With the barest minimum of dialogue and stage directions, create a full dramatic scene that conveys story, situation, character, and so on, and that leaves the door open to the next scene. Consider a scene that begins with a woman screaming, "Get out, you two-timer!" accompanied by a barrage of dishes, silverware, and photos with the man she's yelling at onstage. He's ducking and protesting his innocence until one of the objects she throws tells the man that she's gotten her information from a totally unreliable source (i.e., he sees an object he knows belongs to the jealous neighbor downstairs, though the meaning of this object is not revealed until the next scene).

SEE ALSO: Behavior to Inevitable Words, Disaster, Emotional Winds, Extreme Mood, Familiarity Etude, Mystery Imposition, Short Forms, Stage Directions Only.

MacGuffin

The MacGuffin is the invention of film director Alfred Hitchcock. It could be defined very basically as the false trail that leads to the real story. The most famous example is in his film *Psycho*. We follow the crime committed by Janet Leigh, thinking we're in this fairly routine film about a good woman gone bad because of love, only to discover that the true story centers on a psychotic serial killer named Norman Bates after she's brutally murdered in the shower.

Hitchcock has the MacGuffin lure us in, lull us a bit, and/or set us up for the real story's knockout punch. This etude utilizes that approach from a somewhat different perspective.

The Etude

With either an extant play that seems flat or a new plot you haven't scripted yet, invent a MacGuffin to take the audience into the story from an oblique angle. For instance, if your play is about a formerly abandoned son come to take revenge on the parent who left him behind, you might want to set up a MacGuffin so the story seems to be about a domineering father and an ineffectually rebellious other son (my play called *Blood Relations* took this very approach). An oblique beginning intentionally misdirects the audience so that the impact of the "real" plot is that much greater. We already lack sympathy with the father because of his manipulation of the weaker son and the arrival of this stronger and far more threatening son throws our sympathies into chaos, pulling us further into the issues of the play.

As with all etudes, the caveat is that this exercise may not work for every plot application. Even so, it's a fine exercise for strengthening your approach to a given plot, and I've found it extremely useful many times as a way to just start a play when I haven't a clue where to begin. The MacGuffin etude suggests that you can begin virtually anywhere. If you're clear on how the play ends (or what the middle is about) but are clueless about a beginning, this exercise will provide you with methods of launching yourself. Trust your intuition and start where your first idea points you. In the postexercise analysis you may find that this is not the best beginning. But you're writing to solve the problem rather than sitting around rejecting idea after idea for the "perfect beginning."

The potential of this etude for structural experimentation is also strong. There's no reason why we have to tell our stories from Monday through Friday consecutively, and there's also no reason why we have to tell only character A's story on Monday when telling B's as well will lead us into a more intriguing and complex texture. The MacGuffin will permit you to decide if you want to tell Elaine's story on a bad Wednesday and let that lead backwards to Molly's story on an even worse Monday so we can then leap forward to a disastrous Saturday for both at the clinic where they work. I think the more we can kick theatre off a linear track the better, and the MacGuffin makes a great boot.

A wholly different outcome of this etude may be the discovery that you have an even larger or more complex plot than you initially imagined. Who knows, maybe you even have a trilogy on your hands.

Lastly, the MacGuffin has a direct link to the Entrances and Exits etude, so you should read that etude. The two in combination give you still more possible variations to play with. Other blends would give you very different kinds of bases on which to construct a MacGuffin.

SEE ALSO: Age Explorations, Comings and Goings, Disaster, Emotional Reversal, Entrances and Exits, Free Time, Get-in-Late/Get-out-Early, Mystery Imposition, Normal Day, Other Attribute, Personal Problem, Personal Quality, Place Explorations, Secret Behavior, Secret Objective, Secret Past, What Do I Do for a Living?, and Where Do I Live?

Neuroses

The Neuroses etude offers ways of looking at plot possibilities through character. This is an important perspective to explore because while plays usually can be described as plot-driven or character-driven, it is always story that's at the heart of most theatre, even if by "story" in a given play we mean a collection of images and impressions and not a linear narrative. A character-driven piece focuses largely on the personality of the main character. Her drive to achieve her objective(s) provides the motor or main energy for the play. In this kind of work, the plot is usually a progression of stories and examples that reveal the essence of the character and give an overall sense of the person's life and travails. Plays such as A Streetcar Named Desire, The Little Foxes, or The Transfiguration of Benno Blimpie are good examples of character-driven material.

Neurotics can be loosely defined for our purpose as people who are emotionally unstable, but instability can range from the very complex to the very simple. Mental difficulties can go from all-out phobias (i.e., agoraphobia, claustrophobia, or the fear of flying) to minor obsessions such as having to have a neat desk or retying a tie a dozen times until it's perfect to simpler, more common conditions such as a constant dissatisfaction with your body or facial features. Theatrical neurotics are more often representative of types of conditions, such as Blanche DuBois, Birdie, or Benno Blimpie. Such compulsions and self-deceptions form the basis for archetypes from whom audiences can draw potent analogies, lessons, and images. In this etude you search for unusual character elements that might suggest themselves as plot material.

The Etude

Create or borrow from life a character who is neurotic in some way. It's up to you how strict you want to be about definition; I'm using neurosis in a very general way here to describe people who are functioning in unorthodox ways.

Your primary goal with this exploration is to discover the essential story of this person and her neurosis. This search may lead you to a plot; it may lead you to the back story for a plot. You need to stay open to what the material and your writing process are telling you.

Be willing to explore a variety of personalities in order to discover a range of plot possibilities unless you are using this etude to explore a specific individual. You will also need to keep your objectivity intact throughout the exploring and writing process, since the choice of neuroses you make might be wonderfully self-revealing—a grain of salt and a full dose of your sense of humor are vital to this etude.

SEE ALSO: Best Friend, Emotional Reversal, Extreme Mood, Familiarity Etude, Normal Day, Other Attribute, Personal Problem, Personal Quality, Problem-Solving Monologue, Secret Behavior, Secret Objective, Secret Past, Spoken Subtext, Vocal Distinctions, and Word Choice.

Newspaper

Newspapers, magazines, TV, radio, and the Internet's news and features, should be very obvious plot mines. All have more possibilities than the literal ones we might first assume such as scanning the media on a daily basis for stories with dramatic potential. Less-obvious approaches are detailed below.

The Etude

Shop in the media for story ideas that strike a dramatic chord in you. Once you have a story that intrigues you, write the story in a dramatic fashion. For instance, you may want to track a series of stories from over a period of time in back issues of a newspaper or magazine. This is a bit more difficult to do with TV or radio, but many stations or networks will provide transcripts of broadcasts for a fee, and there are various other sources, such as media museums and public watchdog groups, through which back broadcasts can be viewed. Whether you use a single story or track one through its full run, the basic effort in this variation is to be faithful to the facts and spirit of the story. Seek permission for the rights to tell an exact story or alter the truth sufficiently to fictionalize real events.

Another approach would be to use only the fragment of a story, rather than a whole story as the kick off for an exploration. There was a horrible story in New York years ago about a jealous lover who discovered his girlfriend with another man at a local club. The offended man went to a nearby gas station, bought gasoline, and set the club on fire. Because the club did not meet safety standards and one fire exit was chained shut, many people died. There are many stories in this terrible incident. Think about the murderer, the girlfriend, the club owner, the fire inspector, the innocent victims, the families of the victims, the people in the neighborhood who knew the place was a firetrap but patronized it anyway, and so on. Choosing which stories you wish to tell is based largely on what moves you the most in the story.

Another angle would be to use only the essence of a given story. A playwright in residence at PlayWorks '95, Lisa D'Amour, was developing a play with the working title of *Bad Brains*. It very loosely concerned the childhood of Linus Pauling, the eminent scientist and humanitarian. This very fanciful and beautiful play was based on D'Amour's chance reading of a brief biographical sketch of Pauling in an obituary. The story she crafted became a fable about science, mysticism, feminism, and the spiritual inheritance of family at the turn of the last century and—allegorically, of course—at the turn of this century as well. It is not a literal biography and not meant to be. She wrote a free and intuitive interpolation of the resonances of a life.

I'd recommend you try all three of the variations above to stretch your storytelling perspective, but however you approach this etude, avoid being literal about a source. And don't be too concerned about what a "good" source may be. For example, don't think of daily newspapers only. There are all kinds of newspapers, such as trade papers, grocery store trash, and the multitude of specialty magazines on tattooing, plants, computers, and bass playing. I've also found of great interest the small town and community weeklies that carry tons of local interest stories and great police blotter sections as well as lots of fun photos of area events. Be willing to search for other off-beat choices like public access cable channels, which often feature stranger-than-fiction people and shows.

Yet another unorthodox choice would be to watch shows in an unfamiliar language. Living in El Paso, for example, I often watch chunks of Spanish language shows just to try to guess what's going on (and to get more insight into this amazing border culture). There's also a German language radio show on our local National

Public Radio affiliate that fascinates me. I can't follow the speech at all, but the music choices range from oompah bands to some very interesting rock.

Our world is bombarded daily by these media, so much so that we've stopped paying attention at times. Turning your creative capacities loose in the midst of this bombardment is not only a way of discovering plots for exploration or use, but a manner of making a rational response to it all.

SEE ALSO: Adapting to the Stage Etudes, Being There, Composing to Music, Cross-Cultural Etude, Film Reversal, Found Situations, Oral History, Photo, and Prop Etude.

Obstacle Exercise 1

In theatrical terms, an obstacle prevents a character from obtaining an objective. Hamlet sets out to revenge his murdered father but does not act for numerous reasons (his age, the fact that the revenge would be regicide, the difficulties within the kingdom itself, his mother) that constitute obstacles to his carrying out the planned objective.

Many plays I've read in the past decade have had a significant lack of obstacle as a root problem. These plays tend to focus on a prior event a given character can't seem to get past—guilt plays, I call them. It's true that the guilt—"I forgot to feed the goldfish and it died," "I never called her," or "I never told him how I felt"—is a kind of obstacle, but it can keep the play from moving forward dramatically because the character's entire present is an investment in the past. Arthur Miller, who does guilt better than most playwrights ever have, found solutions to this kind of problem by placing the old guilt up against a new set of problems that cannot be resolved until the old guilt gets punished, forgiven, or vanquished. *All My Sons*, *A View from the Bridge*, and *After the Fall* are prime examples. However, not many writers know how to do what Miller does in his work.

Creating undramatic obstacles is so pervasive, I've heard of playwriting teachers who forbid students to use exposition of any kind in their plays: everything must happen in the present moment and be based on a present problem. Although I find that a bit limiting as a rule of thumb, I like it as an exercise and incorporate the idea here.

The Etude

Write a scene based entirely on a clearly defined obstacle occurring in the present. The obstacle must be something affecting the characters in the scene or that will affect them as a result of the scene. For instance, if you're writing a scene about a man trying desperately to get to a crucial job interview who is confronted by a worker in his apartment building who speaks limited English, you have a very potent obstacle to play with, providing you've set up the objectives well, of course. The job interview character must be absolutely set on making that interview on time, while the worker character must be equally set on completing the very first repair job she's been sent to do. An additional obstacle will help here if the item the worker's been sent to fix—the toilet, say—goes haywire just as the scene begins. Now you have a dual need for the job interview character—to get to the interview, and to get the toilet fixed—and a huge obstacle: a worker who's eager to be of service but cannot understand what's needed. To what lengths will the primary character go to to get to the interview without sacrificing the repair job?

Another example of the low-obstacle plots that I've read is the strangers-meeting-someplace-and-telling-their-entire-life-stories play: The unloved women on the subway platform, the shrink and the closet alcoholic in the stuck elevator, the successful business woman and the bag lady, and so on. Usually, the chief obstacle is that the characters don't know each other, and the usual turn is they discover something in common: "Oh! You carry broccoli in your jacket pocket, too!" usually followed by a laugh and a "moment of recognition." And from this specious point, they proceed to divulge their deepest truths.

Since it's possible that people could behave this way, why not treat it with dramatic respect and continue to provide layers of obstacles? Otherwise, the plot remains only a manipulation of the writer's wishes, bypassing the needs of the characters and the intel-·ligence of the audience.

Challenge yourself to write a strangers meeting scene entirely in the present (no long stories of past tragedies) and to make sure that any level of deepening confidentiality is preceded by credibly overcoming all obstacles to that deepening.

Keep in mind that there are many kinds of obstacles (including actual physical barriers—see Obstacle Exercise 2). Discovering a difficult truth about someone; confronting religious, philosophical, or political values; or simple personality conflicts are all good candidates.

Variations

If you want to write a scene in which the obstacle is a past event or circumstance, try writing the original situation first to see how it happened and how (and why) it will manifest itself in the future.

Another approach would be to reassess plays you've already written in terms of obstacle. You could simply reread the plays or rewrite scenes from a given play to provide a stronger obstacle than you originally created.

SEE ALSO: Behavior to Inevitable Words, Comings and Goings, Entrances and Exits, Extreme Mood, Familiarity Etude, Ground Plan Collaboration, Obstacle Etude 2, Personal Problem, Personal Quality, Secret Behavior, Secret Objective, Secret Past, and Status Etude.

Obstacle Exercise 2

This version of the etude is much more of a game, although it has applications to plot.

The Etude

Create a literal physical obstacle the characters must deal with in the scene you're writing, such as a wall, locked door, dead body, flood, pervasive stench, or any other thing your mind can conjure. This approach somewhat overlaps with Disaster, although the distinction would be based on a matter of degree. If the physical obstacle is a huge heap of running shoes that have suddenly come to life, we're not exactly in a real disaster, but we definitely have a situation.

The main pursuit is to see what happens to your characters when this physical obstacle is imposed. You can either have the physical obstacle present at the beginning of the scene, incorporate it into the scene later on, or even drop it into the scene out of the blue. You could even make a list of physical obstacles on notecards and deal yourself a continual set of problems just to see how the characters cope and what it does to their objectives. And that, of course, is the key: your characters must have strong, clear-cut objectives that they intend to follow through on, no matter the obstacle.

Also, keep in mind that a physical obstacle could be something more subtle than a wall or running shoes. Don't be hesitant to explore as wide a range of possibilities as you can to see where they'll take you.

This etude has application largely to new work you're writing for the exercise, but it can be used for rethinking or shaking up an existing plot or scene. If your tragically opposed father and son are suddenly invaded by giant soap bubbles, what happens to the scene? Could what's tragic about them become even more manifest because of the imposition of something absurd? The soap bubbles may not be the literal choice you'd make in a rewrite but something this outrageous may free you up to find another more organic tack that will have the intended effect.

SEE ALSO: Behavior to Inevitable Words, Being There Etudes, Comings and Goings, Disaster, Entrances and Exits, Extreme Mood, Familiarity Etude, Ground Plan Collaboration, Obstacle Etude 1, Personal Problem, Personal Quality, Place Explorations, Secret Behavior, Secret Objective, Secret Past, Site-Specific, and Status Etude.

Oral History

Oral history has evolved in the last few decades as historians, anthropologists and others have begun to realize that crucial forms of personal documentation (i.e., letters, diaries, journals, and vanity publications) are produced much less often than they once were. Where people once wrote long letters or journals detailing their trip across the plains in covered wagons, today we make a phone call or send each other greeting cards and postcards—and certainly fewer of us keep journals. Oral historians document personal histories on tape and transcripts and preserve these records in archives so that a researcher could discover what one person experienced during World War II or as a child during the Depression.

You can use this etude to discover potential plots by doing oral histories with friends and family, and then fictionalizing the story in a play. You can also use the oral history to build the exposition or background story or even create a documentary drama, as Emily Mann has done with *Execution of Justice*, *Still Life*, and other works. All three approaches have their pitfalls of course, but each can provide you with an actual plot about real events and a plot to play with just for the exercise (see also the Restructuring etude in Chapter 7).

The chief caveat with this etude is that you must be willing to be a neutral interviewer who has no agenda and who permits the interviewee to respond truthfully. These tend to limit your questions to short encouragements such as: what did you do, how old were you, where was this, what did you think, or how did you feel. The worst thing you could do would be to behave like countless TV interviewers who try to make the subject say things emotionally (such as "Tell us how awful you felt then") or to confess or reveal secrets. Oral history may not always be the most scintillating material but this doesn't invalidate it. Your objective is to allow the person to articulate a remembrance.

You should probably limit yourself to audiotaped interviews and avoid video. People are often far more self-conscious with a camera but tend to forget a little tape recorder. If you have subjects who are comfortable in front of a camera, then use it. A record of vocal and physical qualities could be invaluable. In all cases, you should be prepared to provide a copy of the tape to your subject as a form of thanks and "payment."

The Etude
This etude is for finding a new plot or for research and background for an existing play. There are two basic approaches. One is to interview people at random to see if some interesting stories or impressions come from the interview. The other is to interview someone you already know has an interesting story to tell.

The basic procedure begins by conducting the oral history session and then writing a scene or a full piece based on your impressions from the oral history that is coupled with details gathered in the interview. It might be best to start this with someone you know reasonably well before you move on to people you know only slightly or not at all. In every case, you must make clear to the people that you're interested in theatricalizing these stories in some manner. You should probably also tell them that the scene or play you plan to write may bear no resemblance to their actual story; people get oddly possessive about how private affairs are made public even if they've given you full permission.

You may need to conduct a number of sessions with one person to get anything really useful. I did an oral history once with a man, we'll call him Ed, who'd known someone I was interested in, who we'll call Joe, who had died. Hard as I tried to keep the subject on Joe, I soon realized that Ed had many leftover issues with Joe that were going to come up no matter what. My planned study of Joe became an inadvertent study of Ed's unresolved relationship and the way death affects some people. In terms of what is or isn't "useful," you must be careful to stay open to your intuitive side—a single word, image, or story among many will be the trigger that sets a plot loose in your mind.

Variations

Do research for your play with people who experienced the situation(s) in your play, who witnessed the event(s), or who lived in the time of the play. For the sake of broadening your cache of stories, keep a running oral history collection of people you encounter in your daily life. *Stories by the Mailman* may sound of dubious value right now, but who knows?

SEE ALSO: Being There Etude, Character Collaboration, Found Situations, Journal, Newspaper, Oral History, Restructuring, and Site-Specific.

Permission

Permission is the term I use for setting the tone, ambience, and spin at the top of a play. The word refers to literally saying to the audience, "It's OK to take this play this way—in fact, I insist!"

As a director, if I know I'm doing a really scary play, my main objective is to enhance the scariness as strongly as possible in the very first moment of the play (if not in the preset in productions without a curtain). When I directed *The Passion of Dracula*, which opens with a character firing a gun at a bat, the set was lit in preset in very gloomy tones; the recurring decorative motif on the set was owls staring at the audience. The set itself leaned forward a little on the raked stage, and we left the audience in a long, silent blackout after taking the houselights and preshow music out. The gun was fired in this overlong blackout with extra-bright powder. These elements gave the audience permission to be very nervous and ill-at-ease throughout the remainder of the play to better work our other effects on them. Permission means setting the terms of the "deal" of the play by unifying the audience and allowing the production to make the most of that unity.

The Etude

Permission works with existing plays and new pieces. With an existing play, see how many elements you can add to the beginning of the play to set up permission for the audience to connect with the emotions or tone of the play. The purpose here is to find a way to launch the material forward from the strongest base. Too often, playwrights want to spend a lot of time establishing all kinds of things that don't engage us in the play's life. This tendency is probably left over from the old well-made play methods and/or from misapprehending the works of modern masters.

For instance, I often teach *The Glass Menagerie* as a prime example of permission. At first glance, it seems like a play that makes the traditional move of having the first scene set the situation, ambience, and exposition. However, what Williams does in the first scene also gives permission for there to be several layers of reality (Tom's narration, the scrim outer walls, the meal that's eaten with imaginary utensils), lots of room for poetic language and point of view, much irony (Tom referring to the violin playing as "the fiddle in the wings" and Tom and Laura's reactions to Amanda's behavior and stories), and many reminders that what we're seeing is purely theatrical (the slides, the way in which Tom speaks to us and responds to Amanda in a nondirect and scripted way, the outer scrim wall flying out, and so on). All of these elements appear in a very short scene that serves as a brilliant permission for the audience to understand the Wingfield's "normalcy." Without all this permission we could still follow the next scene (Amanda's discovery of Laura's deception) but we'd have so many fewer frames of reference through which to feel and interpret the scene.

In working on your existing play, try to invest the first scene with as much "load" as possible, though you may also try to write a prescene to do the same thing. In working on a new piece, craft the scene with as many levels of permission as you can even if it seems unrealistic or imposed. The main thing is to create the permission in as many ways as you can. You can always go back later and take out stuff that seems implausible.

Again, don't forget that the opening moments of a play are crucial. The audience comes in with its mind on a thousand different realities than that of the play. The more directly, assertively, and clearly you can turn that melange of minds into a single, unified watcher, the better your play's world will succeed.

Variation

Take your existing material, especially unproduced work, to a director (or directors) and have them tell you how she (or they) would stage the opening moments of your play for maximum permission. As a director I have occasionally imposed a scene—a nonverbal one—on the beginning of a play I felt lacked clarity or the kind of spin I wanted to give it. For example, to help establish my interpretation that Tartuffe's man servant Laurent (a silent character) is spying constantly on the family, I needed to create the understanding in the audience's mind that the two men were linked. Otherwise, they had no idea who Laurent was or what he was up to. I created a wordless prescene in which we see Tartuffe directing Laurent to hide on stage just before the ensemble entered. My production may not have been Moliere's *Tartuffe* precisely, but it created the setup I needed for my interpretation of the play. Permission, even when created by the playwright, is interpretation.

SEE ALSO: Behavior to Inevitable Words, Change of Time, Comings and Goings, Entrances and Exits, Filling-in-the-Front, Normal Day, Place Explorations, Restructuring, Secret Behavior, Secret Objectives, Site-Specific, and Stage Directions Only.

Sensory Etude 1: Awareness

Sensory work is the creative process that focuses on a high awareness of the five senses (discussed in Chapter 3). Sensory work simply amounts to paying attention to what all of our senses are taking in at a given moment or to using those same senses to remember an event from the past in the clearest detail.

It takes some work to train yourself to do sensory recall, but it's worth every bit of the effort. Once you've become more adept, you'll realize that we remember exclusively through our senses (though not as strictly through sight as we tend to assume). For example, how often has a song on the radio taken you back to a moment in the past? How many times have scents thrown you into a reverie?

It's through our senses that we most often access the storehouse of our memories, and the unconscious part of us tends to write an ongoing internal narrative as we experience our lives. The four sensory etudes detailed here will assist you when shopping in this storehouse and help you reconnect with that internal narrative. These are ways of discovering plots, though I want to be especially clear that I'm not only advocating autobiographical plots here. This internal narrative includes fantasies and observations of life.

The second aspect of this etude series, the awakening of a sensory awareness in you, will pay off later on. Our senses and sense memories go on without any direct assistance, most often revealing themselves to us in the highly symbolic language of dreams and fantasies. The person who has the ability to tune into this constant stream of input has the highest awareness of her levels of existence and experience.

Lastly, keep in mind that you are an inordinately complex organism, capable of using your senses in ways you may not realize. There's a funny take on this in the film *Bull Durham*, in which the character played by Susan Sarandon helps the character played by Tim Robbins out of his pitching slump by telling him to "breathe through your eyelids," or something to that effect. As he eventually discovers, all she's doing is asking him to focus on something other than his pitching mechanics so that his natural body movements and rhythms will take over.

Although I don't want to scare you away by bounding off into the thickets of non-Western thought, there are philosophies and disciplines that teach us to breathe through our eyelids, hear with our chests, or see through our kneecaps. These are not necessarily just in the realm of intentionally illogical Zen meditations. They fall more into the idea of using our fullest range of sensory capacities to know the world around us. For instance, if you blindfold yourself for a very long time, you will begin to develop the kind of nonsighted sensory tools necessary to navigate a space: you will hear the change in air pressure as you approach a wall or feel the presence of an object as you approach it. Many actors have had training in these kinds of sensory crossover experiences because they awaken the body and mind to many kinds of possibilities. Who is to say we don't listen to music through our shoulders, chests, and legs and not just our ears?

In sum, as you do this work and continue to develop sensory awareness, stay open to what your senses are telling you and stay available to all the kinds of sensory experiences you may have. They might show you whole other ways of looking at plot, structure, and character.

The Etude

In this first version, the purpose is to explore a full range of sensory elements in your work. Create a scene in which all of the senses are utilized in ways crucial to the scene itself. A nuts-and-bolts example would be a scene in which a wine-tasting party is overwhelmed by the sudden intrusion of sewer odors and music so loud it knocks over all the wine glasses; the resultant spilling of the wine then leads to great hilarity because everybody is soaked and wine-dyed and sliding around on the wet floor. In sequence, that scene involved taste, smell, hearing, sight, and touch. The purpose of the scene may be serving as a funny first meeting for the romantic couple of the play, but in the etude you have had the opportunity to involve the senses and create a portion of your plot that might not have occurred to you otherwise.

First attempts may seem forced because your initial etudes might end up being a sort of connect-the-dots exercise as the characters careen from one sense to another. However, there's no reason to separate things—in the example above sight and touch arrived at the same time—and there are absolutely no rules on how you have to evoke the senses. Being so literal as to have characters trying wine in a scene is only one approach to the sense of taste. There's the taste of one's own mouth and the taste of another person's mouth, face, and body. Consider the "taste of fear," the taste of something nasty or wonderful in the air, and so on. Sometimes the audience witnesses sensory elements happening with your characters, and sometimes the sensory elements happen within the characters themselves. When Hamlet talks about "perchance to dream," he is invoking his own inner vision of remembered dreams—he doesn't create a literal visual moment for the audience but he puts us in the context of the visual.

This etude is aimed at starting from creating new material, though there's no reason why you couldn't go back to a scene that seems lifeless and see how sensory work might enliven it.

You could also put together a wide variety of etude combinations here. Imagine moving into a silent situation with Stage Directions Only. I'd suggest that you do all four of the Sensory etudes first, however, before moving off into combinations.

SEE ALSO: Age Explorations, Behavior to Inevitable Words, Being There Etudes, Change of Time, Comings and Goings, Composing to Music, Disaster, Dreams, Emotional Winds, Entrances and Exits, Environmental Etude, Extreme Mood, Fantasy Scenario, Freewriting, Newspaper, Normal Day, Photo, Spoken Subtext, Stage Directions Only, What Do I Do For A Living?, and Where Do I Live?

Sensory Etude 2: Recall

In this version, use a memory of your own to create a scene. This exercise would have no applications for previously written material unless it is already based in the memory you've chosen.

The Etude

Find a place where you can be quiet, relaxed, and concentrated. Select a memory you wish to recall or allow a memory to surface and suggest itself to you. Now focus on recalling as many details of this memory as you can through all your senses. Be sure to have a key event in mind and not just the memory of "the summer of '85" or anything else so general. Also, it's best if the key event had a clear emotional effect on you but wasn't in the realm of the traumatic. As you develop your skills in this discipline, it will be easier to go back to really difficult memories if you wish but I'd thoroughly recommend beginning with lighter emotional events. When you're ready to venture back into difficult memories, you might initially do so with a coach who has some experience in the field.

The easiest way to begin to "do" sensory recall is by sitting comfortably; don't lie down as this invites sleep. Close your eyes and go through your senses one by one: what do I hear, see, taste, smell, and feel in this memory? Give yourself plenty of time to go through each sense and to revisit those which are especially evocative. Don't be a tyrant with yourself if a given sense won't come through. Many people have little recall of the sense of smell, for instance, where for others it's the first sense that arrives every time. You cannot make yourself remember something sensorily—if it's not there, don't worry about it and go on to the next sense. If you leave it alone, a sense may surface on its own.

Once you've had the chance to thoroughly explore the memory, go immediately from it to the place where you write and put the memory down as a scene. Do not write an "I Remember" scene. Develop a scene happening in its own present. Also, do not be too literal about what you're trying to write down in the scene—this is not autobiography but plot exploration—so let your creative powers take over as you continue to draw from your own sensory recall. Write until you've captured the essence of the memory if not the entire experience and then leave the material alone for a day or so.

When you come back, look at what you've written in terms of its faithfulness to the sensory elements (as opposed to the "story," which may have gotten distorted as you interpreted it). Try to get an idea of how the sensory elements first affected you before the writing itself. Lastly, evaluate the material as seeds for a fuller plot.

You can repeat this or any of the sensory etudes as often as you like. I'd recommend them in particular for times when you may be between projects since they're good sources for new ideas, good technical craft-builders, and excellent in general for maintaining an open sensory and intuition system. I'd also urge you to keep a journal record of your sensory work as an annotation of your ideas and experiences. As usual, combinations of this with other related etudes will lead you into many intriguing places.

SEE ALSO: Age Explorations, Behavior to Inevitable Words, Being There Etudes, Change of Time, Comings and Goings, Composing to Music, Disaster, Dreams, Emotional Winds, Entrances and Exits, Environmental Etude, Extreme Mood, Fantasy Scenario,

Freewriting, Newspaper, Normal Day, Photo, Spoken Subtext, Stage Directions Only, What Do I Do for a Living?, and Where Do I Live?

Sensory Etude 3: Enhancement

The shift in this variation and the next is toward emphasizing or deemphasizing the senses intentionally. In order to do either effectively, you should have completed the first two Sensory etudes to gain sufficient grounding in the techniques. Keep in mind that your primary search is for plot ideas and plot approaches.

The Etude

Create a scene in which one of the senses is working far more actively in the scene than the others and see what effect this has on your characters and the situation.

This etude probably has more comic than serious potential at first glance. Certainly a scene in which a character's sense of smell is heightened above all others suggests the likelihood of ridiculous behavior and situations. Even so, we must be careful not to look past the possibilities this somewhat absurd idea presents. For instance, suppose the heightened sense of smell is the condition of a guard in a Nazi concentration camp and this extra awareness leads him to understand with absolute clarity the horror he's helping to perpetrate. Although the main element is fanciful, it still leads us to a dramatic, meaningful place.

This etude will work for newly created material or for rehashing some previously written stuff that seems D.O.A. to you now. In fact, you may find that you're able to rethink an existing scene or play in such an enlivening way that your interest in it may be rekindled.

Variations

Take the heightened sense to an extreme. Suppose your main character felt heat and cold so extremely she couldn't bear to go out or wear clothes. What would happen to her if she were called to Washington to testify before Congress or to receive some major prize in science or the arts? What if she fell in love? How would she consummate a relationship if she couldn't deal with the body temperature of the other person?

A further variation would be to rewrite the same material with a different sense being primary. Yet another would be to combine this immediately with the Age Exploration etudes—what if a thirteen-year-old boy can hear every sound around him? What if a ninety-year-old man suddenly finds the taste of everything an ecstatic experience?

SEE ALSO: Age Explorations, Behavior to Inevitable Words, Being There Etudes, Change of Time, Comings and Goings, Composing to Music, Disaster, Dreams, Emotional Winds, Entrances and Exits, Environmental Etude, Extreme Mood, Fantasy Scenario, Freewriting, Newspaper, Normal Day, Photo, Spoken Subtext, Stage Directions Only, What Do I Do For A Living?, and Where Do I Live?

Sensory Etude 4: Deprivation

I know a woman who lost her sense of smell from a fall. I'd never heard of such a thing until I met her, but such events are not uncommon. We might tend to think of depriving a character of a sense in the "normal" disabilities of blindness or deafness, but what if she lacked the sense of smell, taste, or the ability to feel texture?

The Etude

Create a scene in which a character is deprived of a sense either prior to the scene or during the scene itself and see how this lack affects the nature of the scene. As with Sensory etude 3, you could also try this exercise with existing material to see if this disability would have an interesting effect on any of the characters or the direction of the plot.

Variations

A basic turn on this exercise would be to exaggerate the missing sense in a totally ridiculous way—the character can't see vertical objects and walks into poles and fire hydrants all the time. Or a totally serious way, such as a character who cannot feel pain and so constantly burns or stabs herself without knowing it (as in ALS, usually called Lou Gehrig's disease). Or combine the two. What if a person has no sense of feeling in her body and so can't relate to holding a baby, the pleasure of dancing, or even of stretching herself in the morning?

Another way of extending this would be to link the missing sense to a missing element of a character's personality, such as a man who can see only certain objects because his world view is extremely narrow or because he's a bigot. Again, we must always remind ourselves that when crafting theatre, metaphor is at the heart of what we're doing. Don't be afraid of the images your explorations generate. A different choice would be to combine several deprivations in one character or even to progressively remove one after another until the character is completely bereft of senses.

This etude has most of its application as an exercise with material specifically created from the etude. As previously suggested, however, any etude that will give you a fresh look, even a ridiculous look, at old material is worth trying.

SEE ALSO: Age Explorations, Behavior to Inevitable Words, Being There Etudes, Change of Time, Comings and Goings, Composing to Music, Disaster, Dreams, Emotional Winds, Entrances and Exits, Environmental Etude, Extreme Mood, Fantasy Scenario, Freewriting, Newspaper, Normal Day, Photo, Spoken Subtext, Stage Directions Only, What Do I Do for a Living?, and Where Do I Live?

Site-Specific

This is another exercise courtesy of David Mark Cohen, head of the playwriting program at the University of Texas at Austin. It has many other sources as well, including theatre companies around the world that commission site-specific works based on historic locales.

Site-Specific encourages you to allow an exterior suggestion to direct your intuitive creative responses. It has corollaries in other etudes but the key element of Site-Specific is that what you write must be intended for performance in the site itself.

The Etude

Select a location you feel will have strong suggestive qualities for plot ideas. A museum, for example, has tremendous potential in this regard because it contains so many kinds of provocative images already. However, one can easily go beyond the paintings, photographs, sculptures, or displays of armor and animals and draw from the look of the museum itself, the people who are in the museum, conversations in the cafeteria, and what people are buying in the gift shop.

Once you've gone to the location, the next step is to write a piece that would have to be staged in the site itself. This is the crucial difference between Site-Specific and any other etude based on the observation or inspiration of locale. For example, I saw various presentations of a short site-specific piece called *Sheila's Four O'Clock Tour* by a graduate student at the University of Texas at Austin named Hank Schwemmer. The piece was set in the Archer M. Huntington Art Gallery on campus and is about a guide who goes off the deep end during a particular tour. Seeing the piece performed in different places (first in the museum site and later in a theatre) convinced me that it's truly the connection between material and site that makes the result worthwhile. Although the play still worked on many levels in the second presentation, nothing approached seeing it in its original setting at the museum. Part of this effect came from the intention to be site-specific, but the effect was enhanced even more because of the ambience of the museum, the presence of the actual paintings referred to (largely works by Rothko), and the feeling of being in a "real" tour with tour guide Sheila flipping out on us worked together to create a dramatic "reality" quite unlike anything I'd experienced previously. Being right there was so much more dangerous, ludicrous, and in-on-the-gag than any viewing from the safety and comfort of a theatre seat. Perhaps even more so because some of the "audience" in the museum were unsuspecting citizens who'd wandered onto the periphery of the "tour group" thinking it was real.

I find the idea of creating site-specific material very exciting and challenging. Such material can be approached from any number of angles, one of which would be to write realistically for a site by seeing it, researching it, and investing it with historical accuracy; another would be to use the site as a departure point for a fantasy about the site and ignoring all ties to reality. Start from a sense that the selected site will be evocative for you. There are no guarantees, but always follow your hunches. There's very little to lose in any case.

Begin with spaces that you're familiar with and progress to spaces you do not know. You can store impressions of these spaces for future use in the manner of the Being There etudes, but it's far better to go with the intention of writing something immediately for the space. A fantastic bonus to this etude would be having a production in the space, but keep in mind that's very difficult to do—

getting permission, finding a producer, creating a performance space, and so on, are all tricky but not impossible. It's less difficult as a starting point to do a reading in a site, so don't be totally discouraged by complexities.

SEE ALSO: Being There Etudes, Comings and Goings, Entrances and Exits, Environmental Etude, Oral History, Place Explorations, and Prop Etude.

Situation Exploration

This is a strong etude for plot exploration based on experimenting with characters you have a clear sense of already. This would be particularly useful with characters that interest you but that you have no clear plot for as yet. You might wish to try this etude after playing with some of the etudes in Chapter 5.

The Etude

Place characters you've already developed into a variety of situations they would find stressful. The "situation" can be an unforeseen circumstance such as the characters finding themselves in charge of a group of tourists from another country and not speaking their language or waking up in a strange hotel room with no clothes or money. You could also work on the basis of less far-fetched situations such as the first day on a new job, going on an interview, or planning a proposal for marriage.

While there is some overlap with the etude in Chapter 5 called Disaster, there's a very different purpose with Situation Exploration. In Disaster, you are effectively testing the mettle of a character and seeing how that character would respond to life and death circumstances. In this etude, the exploration is based more on day-to-day stress or on ludicrous or serious crises that are not full-blown disasters. More importantly, this etude is aimed at the discovery of plot possibilities. Disaster can lend itself to finding a plot, but perhaps not quite so readily.

In Situation Exploration, the characters need to be placed in circumstances in which they have to react and try to resolve the difficulty they're embroiled in. You must have them work toward a resolution, but it's not crucial for them to actually arrive. What you're trying to do in this exercise is see what kinds of situations your intuition puts them into and how the effort to solve the situation evolves. Not worrying about the actual final outcome relieves you of concern about a completed plot at an early exercise level; your focus in this etude is on the discovery of plot possibilities that engage your characters in a way you find intriguing and want to continue to play with.

Avoid at all costs the "it was all a dream" or "she's really his sister" kinds of approaches. This is why I'm urging you to avoid worrying about how the situation ends in advance. The learning comes from giving the characters the widest possible range of attempts at solutions. On the other hand, there's no reason why you couldn't combine this exercise with the Dreams etude in this chapter just to keep that predictability factor at bay. However, avoid the trap of a dream solution.

Many other combinations will work as well. This etude is based on the notion of finding plot from an oblique approach. To this end you could also put a variety of situations on notecards and deal them to yourself as you try the exercise.

SEE ALSO: Comings and Goings, Disaster, Dreams, Entrances and Exits, Environmental Etude, Fantasy Scenario, Freewriting, MacGuffin, Mystery Imposition, Newspaper, Notecard Shuffle, Photo, Place Explorations, Problem-Solving Monologue, What Do I Do For A Living?, and Where Do I Live?

Subplot

Subplot is an etude that should be used much more. It instills the kind of discipline that cannot help but enhance your quality of writing.

The Etude

Write a subplot for each of your play's minor characters. The idea here is to create whole lives for all of your characters and to show yourself how a portion of each life intersects with the world of the play and the main characters.

In a way, this exercise is like writing for a soap opera "bible," something that happens for every soap on a yearly (or longer) basis. For a soap opera, the stories of all the characters on the show are worked out in advance. When writers are assigned to write a given segment, they are handed the plot for that show as excerpted from the bible. Their job is to tell that day's plot points through dialogue, images, behavior, and so on. By having a bible to work from, the head writer and the producers of a given soap have total control over the shape of the storylines through an entire year of episodes. All of the twists and turns are worked out in advance. Regardless of my own personal opinion of soaps as a form of writing, I must tip my hat to the creators of these bibles for their ability to plot such complexities so far ahead. It's a staggering task to contemplate.

For our purposes, the notion of filling out the lives of all our characters has several kinds of impact. One kind is keeping us aware of making characters whole and textured human beings. Another kind is ensuring that even the most minor characters in our plays have a more legitimate reason for being present than just serving as exposition tools or other purely functional tasks. A third kind of impact is that giving these minor characters subplots may very well suggest fuller plots for other plays. You may end up providing yourself with material for a trilogy.

As you explore these subplots, keep in mind that you need to avoid making the subplot convenient for intersection with your main plot. If you can stay away from the easy route with this exercise, you'll find that a true life for your characters will begin to emerge in ways you never expected.

For instance, if the subplot for the kid who delivers the telegram in act 2's critical moment is such that the kid has a genuine stake in her own life's needs (such as this is her last telegram to deliver before she starts her new job, goes to college, or goes into the hospital for serious surgery), her life will resonate with the world of the main plot. I do not mean that her subplot must have some impact on the primary story—although that is a choice—I simply mean that what this character has going in her life at that moment affects how she does her task in the life of your play. Maybe she's inexplicably weeping as she hands over the telegram, maybe she's obliviously exuberant as she watches the main character sign what we already know must be a death announcement. It may not be that the arrival of the telegram delivery person is as much a factor to the plot as it is to the tone of the play at that moment. Imagine a party in progress with everyone happy as can be, and this party is interrupted by a weeping telegram delivery person. The telegram may simply tell us that cousin Eddie needs a hundred dollars to fix his car in Omaha, but the impact of this strange outsider may be the very thing that begins a steady shift in tone in your play.

It will probably be easiest to outline the various subplots first and then chart them to see where they intersect with the main plot and develop their impact . You should certainly plan to pursue more depth and theatrical thinking by working these subplots through a variety of other etudes.

SEE ALSO: Blackboard Workout, Character Collaboration, Familiarity Etude, Normal Day, Other Attribute, Personal Problem, Personal Quality, Problem-Solving Monologue, Secret Behavior, Secret Objective, Secret Past, Spoken Subtext, What Do I Do for a Living?, and Where Do I Live?

A final thought before leaving this chapter: because you are a writer, you innately see stories and want to tell stories. However, because you also may be a writer who hopes to be successful, you may be tempted to replicate what has already been done. This year's smash hit will spin off dozens of clones, but remember that there is no formula for what will be the next big success. I hope that doing the etudes in this and the other chapters will encourage you to write your own unique view of the world. Each vision makes our world a larger, fuller place.

7

CHAPTER

Etudes for Structure

AS DISCUSSED IN CHAPTER 6, STRUCTURE IS AN IMPORTANT element of plot. Structure shapes the story and the script itself. Structure is not the what but the how of the story's telling. But because of theatre's nature, the how also becomes the what in a variety of ways. In most cases, the two are completely inseparable.

For example, we all know from the excruciating experience of a confusing joke teller that the shape of a story is crucial: "So, the guy says—oh, by the way, I forgot to mention, he's a traveling salesman—anyway, so the guy says to the farmer—this farmer has a daughter, did I say that already?" The audience usually needs to know certain things first, second, and third for some kind of coherency.

However, there are many other circumstances in which we are perfectly comfortable knowing things third, second, and first as long as the structure sets us up clearly for that kind of progression. A play that requires flashbacks, say, is usually one in which memory is at issue. Other structures focus on other issues. Pinter's Betrayal, for example, relies on a largely reverse chronology to get us to consider much more than just the facts of the story. Because we're aware of moving mostly backward in time, our minds pick up a signal to forego the normal, literal process and opt for a more open and intuitive reception of the story. What's at stake is not how we understand the plot but how we perceive the plot's ramifications. Betrayal's plot is a fairly traditional love triangle, but the nontraditional structure allows us to examine the people in the triangle and how one betrayal has given way to another until we trace our way back to the original betrayal. The structure also reinforces the meaning of the play as the reverse chronology asks us to think more about the ages of the characters and the eras they pass through. Structure, then, sets up perceptions about the given story; it shows us how to see the story and asks us to consider more carefully how we think about that story.

However, structure is also a reflection of the nature of the storyteller. The traditional Western dramatic structure is the essential rising-action-to-an-inevitable-climax found in many classical theorists and playwrights. Modern theatre has come to embrace other kinds of structures. The structures many female writers employ, for example, are less inclined toward the phallocentric pattern of the single climax and follow a pattern I believe is much more related to the female sexual rhythm (or, as others have expressed it, more akin to the female experience of life itself as a pattern of constant interruption).

Non-Western cultures and non-Eurocentric cultures within the West have also contributed varying structural viewpoints and choices. The cyclical nature of many Eastern theatrical forms, for example, has awakened modern theatre artists to possibilities quite different than the traditional model. Certainly Brecht's borrowings from Chinese opera forms showed the way decades ago to a storytelling rhythm quite different from the usual forms of his day and ours. Contemporary theatre practitioners such as the Wooster Group, Mabou Mines, Luis Valdez, Richard Foreman, and Robert Wilson and playwrights such as Maria Irene Fornes, Sam Shepard, Jose Rivera, Mac Wellman, and Suzan-Lori Parks are excellent resources for investigations of structure.

Another aspect of structure has to do with extending the play beyond the basics of storytelling. This includes considerations of structure as rhythm, as a physical metaphor for the story and as a sort of template for the physical realization (sets, lights, and costumes) of the play in production. These terms concern structure as an element of scene length (rhythm), overall shape (physical metaphor), and progression (template).

Scene length is a function of the shape of the play in terms of how much you choose to show an audience at a given time. It is, in effect, your "edit" in the sense of film-cutting. When scenes are written in a short, staccato fashion, the movement of the play is quick and choppy. This rhythm can be continued, aborted, or altered as the play goes on, giving the playwright a great many choices. Having control over the rhythm of the piece gives you ways of using predictability, of lulling the audience or keeping it alert. Awareness of rhythm on the writer's part comes from a sense of theatrical structure as well as the innate structure of the world of the play. This sense is equivalent to thinking of your play as music in the rhythmic pattern of the notes (dialogue) and in the larger rhythmic pattern of the movements (scenes and acts).

The overall shape of your scenes helps to create a physical look to the play itself and to the logical approaches to playing the scenes in sequence. Shape includes such elements as how the scene begins (e.g., in the midst of action or early in the action) and how that scene evolves and where it ends with relation to the next scene. We read, mostly without realizing it, the juxtapositioning and sequencing of the scenes as well as the words and actions within them. In other words, a series of short scenes may look staccato in terms of rhythm, but that may not always be the way to play those scenes once the juxtapositions and sequencing are understood (Fornes's *The Conduct of Life* would serve as a perfect example). A short scene may be broken in many ways with pauses, silences, and freezes as may the moments between the scenes. One scene may introduce an action that is not carried forward until three scenes later, so its particular shape can be described as incremental and like a steadily-evolving collage.

Shape can also include your sense of how you want the material to affect your audience viscerally so that the events and language of these short scenes may be very compressed to give poetic images or fragmented to create a sense of disconnection. By way of example, take a look at a favorite Shakespeare play and compare it to Mamet's *Edmond*. Both move relatively quickly, have fairly short scenes, and the scenes take us from one locale to another, but look at the differences in movement, pace, and impact.

Finally, the shape, rhythm and pace of scenes add up to a progression that helps dictate the physicalization of the play in production—what I'm calling the *template*. We approach styles and genres such as contemporary comedy and classical Greek tragedy from different design values, but we also approach design from a structural appreciation. A modern play with very short scenes occurring in a variety of places and with multiple, interwoven plots tends to be given a design based on speed: unit sets, flexible lights, and quick-change or multiple-use costumes. A modern play with very long scenes in a variety of locales and with multiple, interwoven plots tends to have a more naturalistic design approach. The structure tells the designers that we're going to spend a long time in this one place, so it'll need some details and resonances to help keep that time interesting and vivid.

As a parting perspective on structure, remember that language is also a function of creating structure; the converse is also true. What is said, not said, how things are said, whether what is said is clearly assigned to one character or not, and so on all dictate a sense of structure. Keep in mind that structure refers to how an audience receives a story, receives and perceives the impact of that story, feels and looks at that story, and interprets the intellectual and spiritual realms of that story. Certainly when we enter the world of Heiner Muller's *Hamletmachine* or the worlds of Beckett's plays, we have left behind ordinary logic and therefore the ordinary use of language.

In such works, reality and language are mutable. Often any definite sense of structure—how the story progresses or what world is suggested—is left totally up to the interpreter. Conversely, the language of a naturalistic play such as *Death of a Salesman* actually dictates structure because the language is a clear annotation of very specific mental processes on the parts of the characters. There are only so many ways to approach Willy's repeated lines about being "well-liked," while an actor could invent an infinite number of approaches to Hamm's speeches in *End Game*. While it's true that Willy Loman's sense of reality is highly mutable, his language is based in the same essential reality as our own. Therefore, the play tells us the story of Willy's fall and madness rather than placing us in a more purely symbolic or metaphorical representation of that fall and madness as in *End Game*. Our artistic interpretation when producing these works is to choose a linear storytelling approach to structural values with

Death of a Salesman and a non-linear experiential approach to structural values with *End Game* because the language leads us to do so.

Obviously, structure is a very complex issue. I hope you will pursue further explorations on structure in theory and practice. Reading as many contemporary plays as possible, especially those not in the mainstream, will be very helpful. It's not in the scope of this book to delve more deeply into the theoretical aspects. My primary goal in this chapter is to get you to think about structure in as many new ways as possible on your own. There are many etudes from the other chapters with potential for structural exploration and application as well—especially those focusing on adaptation or on the incorporation of other disciplines such as music and design. What I hope you'll develop as you work through these exercises is a new perspective on structure for discovering alternative approaches to telling the stories you wish to tell. These efforts may, of course, send you back more convinced than ever that yours is the only way, but then you'll have had the chance to consider other possibilities.

A last thought before the etudes: keep in mind that in modern theatre the primary job is not simply reporting a story. That's one kind of playwriting, of course, and not one I'd dismiss. But it is through the dozens of exciting tools largely available only in theatre that playwrights have the chance to "tell the tale" in unlimited ways. My hope is that you will challenge yourself to find new methods of reinventing and reseeing the stage.

KEY ETUDE
Restructuring

This etude is strictly for playing with an existing piece of your own creation. Its primary purpose is to extend your conception of structure by asking you to dismantle the way in which you originally told a story, rethink it, and piece it back together in a new configuration. This process is not as easy as it may sound, so there are lots of caveats to go along with the basic exercise.

The Etude

Choose a play you wrote a while back—one that's got a linear structure—and reread it. Make an outline of the scene sequence and story progression. Take the outline and look at it now with a view toward reshaping the play for a different impact.

Why a play written "a while back"? Because I want you to have come to terms and resolution with the play. The play should be something that you felt good with and not troubled over, and it should not be a piece you're still trying to understand. Above all, it should be a play you have a sense of perspective on so that dismantling it won't disturb you. Keep in mind that you're working initially with an outline anyway, so there should be no actual dismantling of the original script.

In preparing the scene and story outline, you'll need to be very disciplined and deal only with the play as it is. Don't get trapped into thinking ahead to a new structure. Just try to deal with the play as you originally intended it (and actually wrote it). The end result will be vital to the whole exercise, so it's important that you stay faithful to your original ideas and execution.

Once you've completed your outline, the key step will be trying to discover what sparked this play in you in the first place. You need to go back to that inspiration point because it will determine how to restructure the material. For example, say your first hint of the play came through being chilled by an image like a man or woman stepping through an open window onto a ledge on his or her way to jumping. Once you decided to write the play, perhaps your decision was to go back in this person's life and follow a week or a day when everything came apart, leading to the moment to commit suicide. Your outline should then follow a very linear sequence: Character A wakes up, realizes that B has left him for good; tries to get going but can't hack it, and ends up snorting a line of cocaine to get motivated. A has many difficulties getting out of the house and getting to work. At work, A is confronted by C, a former flirtation, who is now planning to sue A for sexual harassment. Later, A is told by D, his boss, that the company tends to believe sexual harassment suits no matter the trial verdict, and A should start looking for another job.

That's your story that leads to the moment of terror and pity: A steps onto the ledge, looks into the abyss, and blackout.

The point of this exercise is to ask you to rethink your reaction to your initial image (by *reaction* I mean the play you chose to write).

In the linear story you chose to create, the function of the structure was in effect to explain what led to A's choice. It could be that you saw the choice as inevitable or as highly preventable: if only A had been more together or the others around A more sensitive. Regardless, the play in its present structure explains or presents a case for the events at the final decision.

At this point you need to challenge your conception of the stimulus image and how to employ it. For example, let's say you might want to ridicule suicide as a choice by showing A heading for the ledge a number of times, each time becoming more absurd. So your play might open with a sort of slow-motion moving toward the ledge and then blackout to the waking-up moment. You might intersperse throughout the sequence of scenes stranger and more ridiculous goings-to-the-ledge: as a ballet, as a robot, as a Charlie Chaplin figure, as an eager diver planning to score that perfect ten off the high board. In this particular restructuring, you've kept your scene order but broken the scenes up with the interscenes that create their own commentary.

You could take advantage of the same structure but with a different purpose by showing the horror of suicide. Such an approach would eliminate the silly choices I've described and focus instead on using the repetition as a way of layering and reinforcing the horror.

A different restructuring might begin with the moment of stepping onto the ledge, then follow the scene sequence backwards until we get to the moment at which A knows he's been abandoned by B, at which point we see the ledge scene again. This sequence would show an entirely different kind of perspective because we'd first suppose A to be just an office letch and then we'd gradually see that he has more problems. You could also follow a sequence of scenes backwards to a key point and then move forward again—it simply depends on what you want to say through the structure.

What we've done up to now is rework the direction (or the repetition) of scenes rather than add entirely new material, but it would even be permissible in the context of this etude to add scenes to rebuild structure. These scenes should be principally flashback or flashforward scenes to provide information otherwise unobtainable.

In any case—and you really ought to try as many kinds of

restructurings as you can—the whole effort here is toward ungluing your work from any kind of "usual" approach. As I said initially, the discovery may be that you still like your usual approach, but at least you'll have looked at alternatives. It's far more likely, however, that a different way of thinking may grow within you to shape a play in order to take the audience to as many levels as possible as opposed to shaping it simply to tell the story.

The extensive etude list below is not a group directly analogous to this etude as would normally be the case but etudes from other chapters I feel have structural applications. Maybe you've done these etudes already and don't need to try them again, but it would be worth your time to take another look at these exercises from this different perspective. For instance, some of the etudes, such as Dreams or the various etudes focused on adaptation, would be excellent exercises for an early exploration of a plot you want to keep from being linear. Etudes such as the Fantasy Scenario may help you find new approaches for the thinking processes of your characters, again freeing you to attack your work from different angles.

Lastly, I would urge you to read as much new work that is nontraditional in style, structure, and content as you can. I mentioned a group of writers above and can add to that list Lee Breuer, Milcha Sanchez-Scott, John Guare, Emily Mann, Eric Bogosian, Christopher Durang, Ntozake Shange, Richard Nelson, Megan Terry, Jane Anderson, Joan Holden, Donald Margulies, Tom Stoppard, Vaclav Havel, and Caryl Churchill. I can guarantee that none of their works will be the usual, well-made pieces that too many of us have allowed to be accepted as standard for too long. I would urge you even more strongly to see nontraditional work whenever you can because it'll challenge your ways of thinking. You should see other forms of performance as well such as modern dance, modern opera, performance art, and one-person shows.

SEE ALSO: Adaptation Etudes, Adapting to the Stage Etudes, Age Explorations, Blackboard Workout, Change of Time, Comings and Goings, Composing to Music, Dreams, Emotional Reversal, Emotional Winds, Entrances and Exits, Fantasy Scenario, Film Game, Film Reversal, Freewriting, MacGuffin, Newspaper, Normal Day, Notecard Shuffle, Other Forms, Photo, Secret Behavior, Secret Objective, Secret

Past, Sensory Etudes, Style Copy, Subplot, Vocal Distinctions, What Do I Do for a Living?, Where Do I Live?, and Word Choice.

OTHER ETUDES
Blackboard Workout

Although similar to the Restructuring etude, the Blackboard Workout has several crucial differences. First, it can be used on a play you're considering, working on, or have just finished. Second, it can be used as a way of looking at other writers' structures. Third, it relies more on a charting of material than an outline method—the structural representation is more visual. Of course, a large drawing pad will work if you don't have a blackboard available, and note-cards can work as well.

The Etude

Using a blackboard, chart the structure of the play you've chosen to examine by plotting the key events of the play along a line on the board. Other elements can be annotations of what each character knows and when and indications of the crisis points in the play.

Try to pay attention to how these elements are progressing—toward a climax, anticlimax, series of climaxes or epiphanies, and so on. This progression can be plotted with a line in the manner of a graph with peaks and rises in the lines to show these moments of higher dramatic impact. You can also help yourself by annotating the duration of each scene in pages or estimated minutes to observe how long each segment is taking. Duration can show, for example, that you're spending 75 percent of your time on character A and only 15 percent on character B when you'd thought they were balanced.

Sit down and take a long look at your finished chart. The line, its elements, and any other notations should help you clearly visualize the progress of the play. You might also get a better sense of how the play flows from one moment to the next, how well the characters are balanced, whether your expositional elements are in the right places, and if your climax is well timed. It will be almost as if you have a conductor's score in front of you and can see more easily the movement of the entire piece. This chart represents your initial investigation of your structure. You might now decide to take this etude to the next level by using the Restructuring etude.

With a large surface like a blackboard, you can easily move things around to study the impact on flow and story clarity. However, be careful not to lose track of the original structure. For instance, I have had the luxury of classrooms with more than one blackboard, which permits me to work from one chalked picture that doesn't get altered to another that does. Whatever you can do to prevent inadvertent erasures will be helpful, and any situation where you can easily view two structures (or more) side by side is ideal. If you have no blackboard available, using a large drawing pad would be the best alternative. Try pulling each page out and mounting it on a wall: you need to create some physical distance for yourself in order to truly see the characteristics of your structure and restructure(s).

Variations

Plot all of the characters through the play and where they interact with each other; plot the placement of dialogue and monologues to see if you're setting up a rhythm that's not intended; plot the locations. Another approach is through the use of French scenes, which is a method of annotating the beginning and end of scenes strictly by the entrance or exit of one or more characters. It's the style used by Moliere and his contemporaries and can be very helpful to you because it will allow you to think of the play less in terms of dramatic beginnings and endings (i.e., the traditional scene structure), and more in terms of the movement of characters and their interaction. This approach is helpful especially for farce since one of the keys to this comic style is who knows what and at what point. I'd suggest looking at a modern adaptation of Moliere (Christopher Hampton's adaptation of *Tartuffe* is especially readable, since he opted to move away from the cumbersome rhymed couplet style). Converting a play into French scenes is often done for scheduling rehearsals as well because it gives you a more accurate picture of which characters are needed when.

SEE ALSO: Cross-Cultural Etude, Notecard Shuffle, Other Era, Other Forms, Restructuring Etude, and Style Copy.

Cross-Cultural Etude

This is an excellent exercise for rethinking your approach to structure, and for introducing yourself to the writing, concerns, and structural modes of other artists on the planet.

The Etude

Find plays written in the traditional forms of other cultures, and study them closely as to the manner in which structure, plot, character, and other elements are handled. You might want to read about the rules and customs that influence the style and structure of the plays first to have a better appreciation of the material before reading, especially since some forms like Noh and Kathakali can seem impenetrable on first look. For plays and studies related to Asia, the University of Hawaii Press is excellent; for plays and studies related to Africa, the Middle East, and South America, look to Heinemann, Routledge, and Grove Press among others. You can also consult your library and other catalogue sources. You might also want to look for videos of performances from other cultures, which can be even more enlightening. Some video catalogue sources are listed below.

Another approach would be to examine the plays (and evaluations and criticisms of them) from the experimental theatre of the United States, Europe, and Japan. This exercise is cross-cultural in the sense that such "fringe" theatre comes from its own unique political, economic, and social orientations as much as does the theatre of any other group foreign to your mainstream. A while ago, I found a copy of *Dionysus in 69*, the legendary performance piece done by the Performance Group in New York, while I was in a used book store in Fayetteville, Arkansas. Before reading the play, I thought that I knew a great deal about it—I certainly knew the work of the Performance Group from seeing them and reading about them, and I'm familiar with other such experimental companies— but I was completely wrong; the piece was far more ambitious and exciting than I'd thought, particularly in the sense of the material as a document of its period and of that period's world view. I learned a great deal from studying this piece, especially about making assumptions. There aren't a tremendous number of scripts available for this kind of material, but even reading about the performances can be very enlightening.

Seeing these pieces in performance can also be eye-opening. There are a variety of sources for videos, such as Mystic Fire in Michigan ([800] 292-9001), Art Com in San Francisco ([415] 431-7524), and

Viewfinders Uncommon Video in Illinois ([800] 342-3342). For a broad study of experimental theatre in this country, one of the best sources is *American Alternative Theatre* by Ted Shank (New York: St. Martin's Press).

Once you've had a chance to read plays from other cultures, you should try writing your own version. This exercise is similar to the Style Copy and Other Era etudes below except that here you are investigating how to adapt your own material in another culture's perspective and methods as opposed to a more literal aping of a given writer's voice. Your attempt may present you with some really unique challenges to your writerly process.

For instance, I had a wonderful graduate student named Jim Utz who wanted to write a modern Greek tragedy using as many elements from Aristotle as possible. He spent a semester reading the Greeks very intensively and then turned toward the process of creating his modern version of a Greek tragedy. His first and most difficult problem came from the recognition that the modern American heterogeneous culture and the ancient Greek homogeneous culture have very little in common. His ultimate solution was to create a fictional state called Lweezyana (also the title of the play), which had broken off from the United States in a revolution of African Americans who wanted their own nation. In this new nation it was possible to have a homogeneous society, a king and queen (a necessary element for classic tragedy, of course), and a unique style of language that included choral odes based on religious influences and musical traditions from jazz and the blues.

Utz's highly creative use of his own roots helped him to find a way of approximating a culture from another time and place. I know this had (and will continue to have) a profound effect on his writing process, and I believe it had an even more important impact on his own world view.

SEE ALSO: Adaptation Etudes, Adapting to the Stage Etudes, Blackboard Workout, Oral History, Other Era, Site-Specific, and Style Copy.

Flashbacks and Flashforwards

Some of our structural sensibility is derived from our sense of time. Most of us learn about time as a continually moving-forward abstraction represented by the hands of a clock or a digital readout. We tend to think of time as a representation of the past, present, or future. Some cultures think about time as a representation of past, present, and future simultaneously. There are other cultures that believe in parallel times, so that this moment represents itself and the one next to it, and the one next to that, with our various lives all occurring at the same instant. It's possible that we can express these kinds of time-views as related to the more modern concepts of the conscious and unconscious parts of ourselves, but that may be just an explaining away of the magical potentials of time. However you view time, you can investigate the possibilities of theatrical time through this etude in order to liberate your use of time onstage.

The Etude

Work on a new play in which the story you want to tell is developed through the use of flashbacks and flashforwards. (It's possible to do this exercise with an existing play, but it seems like more fun to work from scratch.) In the process of creating this play, you have various options. One option is to make the shifting from present to past to future obvious and delineated in some fashion. Another is to create the shifts without clear demarcations. In the first case, you are showing an audience the past and future in a way that essentially explains or comments on the present. In the second, you are blurring the lines to say there is no difference or that explanations are unnecessary. These options are not the only statements you can make in playing with these time shifts; I include them only as examples for you to make use of or depart from. However you approach this exercise, you need to remember that you're experimenting with the impact of time, time shifts, and your own sense of time and its values.

There are an infinite number of applications to this exercise. For instance, one project would be to write a play in which a person in the present has no memory due to psychological blocks or terrible childhood experiences but who, due to the onset of brain-damage or some other condition, can *only* recall the horrors of childhood in old age. This is a very literal use of time shifts, in which past meets future. A differently literal application would be to write a play in which someone is involuntarily shifting through time—a sort of science-fiction play that could have social, political, or historical meanings.

A very different example is seen in a play called O.T., written in residence by Clay Nichols in the PlayWorks Festival at the University of Texas at El Paso. In this play, a man is trying to prove that his girlfriend's assessment of him as a political and social throwback is wrong and so he's taken on a big brother-style commitment to a disadvantaged kid. One of the elements of the play's structure is that the audience sees in the first act the growing problems in the couple's relationship (shown through present-time and flashback time intermingled) and the difficulties with the big brother relationship side by side as if they're happening in the same time, only to discover later on that the two relationships are happening at separate times. Nichols's use of time and his deliberate confusion of the audience form a metaphorical statement in the play that suggests that we often make distinctions about ourselves based on personal chronology, but who we are is in constant flux, and that the past is always with us.

These are just a few examples of how you can play with time to create story ideas and learn about structure and to have a structure make statements beyond the literal surface of the story. Your inventions and improvisations on the basic ideas outlined here will no doubt carry you forward into some very intriguing possibilities. I'd suggest the following brief reading list: *Fool for Love* by Sam Shepard, *The Danube* and *The Conduct of Life* by Maria Irene Fornes, *The Glass Menagerie* by Tennessee Williams, *Equus* by Peter Shaffer, *Cloud Nine* by Caryl Churchill, *A Bright Room Called Day* by Tony Kushner, and *Assassins* by Stephen Sondheim and John Weidman.

A final thought: don't worry about being too literal about past, present, and future. You could easily mean now, five minutes ago, and five minutes from now as your time frames. Again, the point is to have control over time as a tool, metaphor, and statement in your work.

SEE ALSO: Age Explorations, Blackboard Workout, Change of Time, Comings and Goings, Cross-Cultural Etude, Dreams, Entrances and Exits, Notecard Shuffle, Other Era, Secret Past, Sensory Etudes, and Site-Specific.

Mystery Imposition

The technique for this etude is to force a play's plot and structure into the standard style of a detective story (or into other familiar genres as suggested in the variations). This etude may seem to have a relatively frivolous approach to structure, but the exercise will have many benefits for you.

While my description may sound like you are simply imposing one style onto another, you will certainly learn how to avoid being stuck with plays that arrive at big revelations. Most such plays rely on the hidden existence of some horrible, shameful past deed or oversight, so they're largely about guilt and denial. They are, in effect, detective stories ("We're in search of the truth of this past event") but often without any of the fun of detective stories. The Mystery Imposition etude puts the fun back in while knocking a for-mulaic approach out of kilter.

You will note similarities with the Adaptation etudes and the Adapting to the Stage etudes. However, here you impose a genre or form onto your own play. You'll find the results quite different.

The Etude

Treat your play as a mystery, whether the piece is an existing script or one you'll write for the exercise. If you're unfamiliar with the stan-dard detective story or mystery form, try reading some Dashiell Hammet, Mickey Spillane, or Raymond Chandler to get a sense of the writers whose styles helped form the genre from the 1930s through the 1950s. There are other stylists such as Jim Thompson or Cornell Woolrich, among others, whose harder-boiled school of *noir* styles put part of the genre into another league altogether. There are also a fair number of plays available with this basic style including *Ten Little Indians*, *Sleuth*, and Eric Overmyer's treatment of the genre *In a Pig's Valise*. There are many good films: *The Maltese Falcon*, *The Big Sleep*, *The Thin Man* series, *Chinatown*, and *The Usual Suspects*.

However, to save a little leg work, here's the essential formula: a crime is committed and the detective seeks to solve it. In the process, dark and strange things usually emerge about the people involved in the case, and these dark and strange things normally challenge the belief system, moral code, world view of the detective or an innocent party caught up in the maze (although, as the form evolved into modern and postmodern modes, there were no inno-cents to be found anywhere). In the end, the solution—who done it—is far less relevant than the issue of the detective's or innocent's state as a result of having been exposed to the darkness and strangeness of the case. In other words, the detective story is a kind of MacGuffin (see this etude), or excuse to tell a story about the hidden aspects of human nature.

A simple approach is to invert the usual revelation-at-the-climax approach to playwriting by placing the revelation—or climax—at the beginning. In the literal world of the mystery, the whole process is kicked into gear by the appearance of the murdered person. In our figurative use of the mystery, the corpse can be anything that will be the lynchpin for the larger story we want to tell.

As an example, let's examine the following story: Scene 1: John jilts Mary at the altar. Scene 2: Mary confronts John's brother Bill to find out where John is and why John did it. Scene 3: A flashback that begins with Bill's narration. We now have a scene in which John and Bill are teenagers. In this scene we come to understand that John has been sexually ambivalent for much of his adolescence. Scene 4: Back to Mary and Bill; Mary wants to know how John could still have this "problem" when she and John have had a great relationship. Scene 5: Another flashback in which we see John at twenty-one falling madly in love with George, who eventually leaves him; John foreswears his homosexuality. Scene 6: Two years later, just before the wedding, John is riding along toward the church with Bill. John is nervous but happy. He suddenly sees George on the street. And so on.

Now, this may seem pretty corny as a plot but how is it less corny than the play in which John and Mary are seemingly happily married but things have gotten bad lately and it all comes out in the end that John led a life of false heterosexuality, accompanied by long, and tortured confessional speeches? You may disagree with my perspective of course, but my feeling is that the story told through shifts of time and in pursuit of an active solution to a known problem is more interesting. In the end-revelation formula, the audience is most often told the Terrible Truth, which makes the audience passive and treats it condescendingly. In either case, we're learning about a hidden aspect of the character; the issue, for me, is how we're learning—actively or passively?

At any rate, as always the purpose is to re-invent ourselves and our approach to crafting plays; it may be that my suggested

detective format doesn't quite hit the mark for you but instead triggers some other kinds of ideas about styles, genres, formats, etc.,
and that would be perfectly wonderful.

Variations

Some basic variations to this etude would be imposing TV sitcom or
B-horror movie styles. What would happen to the structure of your
play if you imposed a basic I *Love Lucy* structure? After all, the formula is very basic: dangle before the main character a carrot he is not
"allowed" to have and let him try to find the most devious but funny
way of getting at the carrot that turns the situation into mayhem.

Keep in mind that there are other aspects to consider as well
as the basic form. In the case of the *Lucy* series, much of the basis
of the show was based on the dilemma of women in an era when
they had no power. In other words, Lucy had to be devious. Perhaps
your choice of style to impose on the material will suggest analogs
to you about your material worth noticing. For instance, if you chose
a *Lucy* format, would this be because the character you're focused
on is also powerless in some way? Always trust your intuition and
try to make a habit of doing some postanalysis.

There are numerous styles to choose from that I needn't bother
suggesting here since the choices will (and should) come from your
sense of your own play. It may be that you'll want to impose a variety of styles on the play to see what happens as each style affects the
structure of the original material. There's no need to write these out
fully; it will be just as useful to play with the style imposition in an
outline format or by using the Blackboard Workout technique.

Lastly, remember that this etude may have added value to you
for technique, plot, character, or writer's block because other genres
are often so evocative. Start from structure and follow your nose.

SEE ALSO: Adaptation Etudes, Adapting to the Stage Etudes,
Cross-Cultural Etude, Film Game, Film Reversal, Flashbacks and
Flashforwards, MacGuffin, Notecard Shuffle, Other Era, Secret
Behavior, Secret Objective, Secret Past, and Style Copy.

Notecard Shuffle

As a fun way to shake up your normal sense of structure, the
Notecard Shuffle brings sheer whimsy and chance to your process.

If you're not a fan of the serendipitous, this etude is probably not for you. You'll need a sense of humor, a lot of patience, and a willingness to be open minded.

The Etude

Outline a play you're currently working on or one you've previously written by placing each important plot element on a notecard. The number of cards depends on how fine a point you wish to make of the plot elements. You could have a hundred cards for a very complex one-act or only fifty for a two-act play. Less is more, but you wouldn't want to find yourself with only five notecards either. The ideal number will evolve for you after trying the etude a few times.

Once you have your notecards in sequence, use a blackboard or drawing pad to put the same outline into an easily seen format. Then, throwing logic to the four winds, shuffle the cards.

What you'll probably have is a ridiculous mishmash of plot elements falling in all kinds of weird configurations. Even so, write out this new outline and see what you have.

This brings us to the most crucial step. Take a close look at this outline and see if there are any elements in a new sequence that might be more interesting. If anything strikes you as intriguing, make a note of it next to the outline on the blackboard or drawing pad and shuffle again. You can repeat this process as many times as you'd like, just to see where things land.

At a certain level, this is the equivalent of throwing the I *Ching* or following one's astrological readings. It may be too mystical for some people, and that's fine. The point is simply learning how to unthink your old methods and rethink your way to new ones. It is just as likely that absolutely nothing of value or interest will come out of this etude as it is that some major epiphany will occur. To my way of thinking, the purpose is not to "get" a new structure but to set your mind free of its normal processes in search of other ways of assessing and investing in your work.

When I'm working on a new play, friends will ask how things are going. Sometimes I'll say great, terrible, or "who knows?" Sometimes I'll say, "Well, I'm just letting the play think about me for a while." This is not an answer that many people are comfortable with. They usually take it as a joke, but I'm serious. My own process is to take an idea for a play and let it incubate for a while—a week or six months—which means letting it reveal itself for a while before committing to the writing process. I'll be worrying about the car or musing about my kids when some image for the play will just present itself. I'll then write notes or do a variety of explorations, just to see how the image manifests itself theatrically. As the play becomes more clear, the interruptions will become more frequent until I'm sufficiently focused to start writing scenes and more dedicated explorations.

Sometimes I'll need to stop working on the play—because life is intruding or I've run into a wall—and that's when this intuitive process takes over once again. This process may take more focused forms at this point though; I might spend a lot of time listening to music that's connected to the play, for instance. No matter what, the play is always talking to me. And the Notecard Shuffle can be really helpful. It's a game of course, and an exploration in randomness, but it is also a meditation and a way of trying to open up as many channels within myself as possible.

Variations

Outline and shuffle only one act at time. Such an approach may be a good starting point for a writer with little or no experience.

Another approach is to put your notecards on a table and make the shifts in structure on purpose to see how the original outline hangs together. Consider having four events in Scene 1

1. X arrives at Y's home.
2. X reveals that he is dying and needs help.
3. Y declines to help take care of X.
4. X reveals that he has always been in love with Y.

Why does event 4 have to occur fourth? What would happen if it were to occur second or third in the scene?

As with most of the other etudes in this chapter, the hope is that challenging every kind of structural decision will develop a more open approach and enhance your craft and thinking processes.

SEE ALSO: Adaptation Etudes, Adapting to the Stage Etudes, Blackboard Workout, Cross-Cultural Etude, Film Game, Film Reversal, Other Era, and Style Copy.

Other Era

This etude and Style Copy have similarities to the Cross-Cultural Etude. Cross-Cultural is an investment in structure as seen by other cultures. Style Copy is a conscious aping of one writer's techniques and choices, and Other Era is an exploration of the impact of historical realities on structure.

For instance, Shakespeare didn't just get it into his head one day to write in iambic pentameter—this limit was set by the style of the time in which he wrote. Similarly, the writers in this country who set the tone for playwriting for many decades—O'Neill, Odets, Hellman, Williams, and Miller—often worked within a set of structural methods that have since been altered (if not altogether discarded) toward yet another set of structural methods.

Knowing how a given era's playwrights structured their work and under what conditions will give you insights into the thinking of a given time period and the creative responses to impositions on thinking.

The Etude

Go back to the work of a favorite playwright whose best work dates from at least fifty years ago. Reread this writer's work extensively and spend some time reading about the writer's work. Focus on analyses of style, structure, methods, and so on. Make sure you understand as fully as possible the conditions under which the writer was working. Once you feel you have a clear sense of this writer's approach and "brush strokes," write your own scene(s) or play based on that style.

There are three key elements to remember. First make as accurate an assessment of the style of your chosen writer as possible. Why did Shakespeare choose to have *Hamlet* structured as he did? Why did Ibsen write A *Doll's House* as he did? There is a wonderful book called *From Ibsen's Workshop*, edited by William Archer (New York: Da Capo Press), which shows Ibsen's notes about and drafts of various plays, the lengthiest of which is from A *Doll's House*. Through such resources, we're able to get a sense of how various writers approached their own work, what they kept and threw out, what they wrestled with to arrive at the play we've come to know. If only more writers held on to more drafts of their plays. Imagine seeing the very first draft of *Oedipus Rex*!

A slightly different angle to work would be looking at your chosen writer and his contemporaries as well to see what the differences are. In any era, there are hundreds of playwrights working—why is it that one or two become the best of that group? What did they do that's so special?

The second element of the etude is trying to ape the style of this era that you've come to understand. Focus on copying one writer's style from the era or on the general style of most playwrights in the era. It's harder and easier than you may realize in many ways, but it will teach you a great deal about the thinking processes of this period. As poet Robert Hass observed on the PBS program *Language of Life,* "When one says somebody else's poem aloud, one speaks in [the poet's] breath." In this case, you would be writing in your playwright's hand and vision.

Consider another take on this second element. Elena Carrillo, a student of mine, was having a hard time making the transition to writing plays from her background of writing novels. She chose to write a play in a Victorian style. Given that her novels were largely written in this same style, I thought her choice was a very smart one because it allowed her to explore a new form in a familiar mode—she knew the era well but not the medium of playwriting. Once she'd found a comfortable world in which to explore playwriting, her progress was remarkable, and she's been one of my most successful playwrights ever since.

Once you've explored this etude, take what you've learned and apply it to your own work. Perhaps it will show you similarities and dissimilarities between yourself and the chosen era that will ask you to rethink your own process. Perhaps you'll find a structure that you'll want to borrow from. Or you'll want to try to find a way of creating a modern version of another culture or era as the starting point for a new play. This exploration will open you up to many new avenues for your work process. If nothing else, it will serve as a reminder that the great playwrights also sat in quiet rooms and sweated out choice after choice for their own works.

A basic and helpful variation would be to outline plays from a selected era on the blackboard to get a sense of how they work. Mechanics learn by taking engines apart and putting them back together, and we can do the same thing for ourselves.

SEE ALSO: Adaptation Etudes, Adapting to the Stage Etudes, Blackboard Workout, Cross-Cultural Etude, Notecard Shuffle, and Style Copy.

Style Copy

Style Copy is a fairly traditional classroom exercise that has a great deal of potential for both technique and applied structural development. The only distinction between it and the Cross-Cultural and Other Era etudes is that your focus is strictly on the style of a single contemporary playwright.

The Etude

Select a modern playwright whose work excites and stimulates your imagination. Reread the work of this playwright as thoroughly as you can to get a sense of the essential style. Write a scene (or more) in that style.

The primary focus is structure, of course. If you're choosing Maria Irene Fornes, for instance, you'll note that in most of her plays the structure is contiguous rather than continuous because she's less interested in chronology than on the impact of specific events and their juxtapositions. You'll also notice that her structure is built on extremely compact scenes and language. Trying to work within the rigor of her style will teach you a great deal about a very individual view of the theatre. Be sure to choose a writer whose style is unique and challenging.

Once you've written the etude, it would be great fun for you to have a group of actors read a selection from the original writer's work, followed by your work to see if you've hit the mark. There are always surprising elements of plays that only come through by verbalizing them. In fact, you would probably gain a great deal from doing this with the Cross-Culture and Other Era etudes as well. No one will be exact in every detail and nuance, of course, but this extension of the etude could be very helpful.

As with the other etudes, trying this first as a Blackboard Workout could be useful. There are a thousand details to anyone's play and style; getting a clear sense of the shape of that style first could open the doors to seeing many other details for you.

Lastly, I would recommend that you copy the style of a variety of writers—particularly writers who represent many differences from your style. There is so much to be learned from the ways of others that it would practically take another book just to develop the possibilities further. Suffice it to say for now that we are in a lucky position in history: we have several thousand years of influences to learn from and draw on, and we are in an era in which politics and social realities have made it possible for people from every conceivable background to write plays.

Variation

Finish a given writer's play or attempt to write the scene(s) that would have occurred before the play began or sometime after it ended. Your choice should be completely intuitive of course, but your postanalysis should include some thought as to why you chose as you did. Had the writer left too much hanging? Did the play seem to lack exposition? Although we're right to venerate our favorite writers, it's important that we not lose our critical perspective on them.

SEE ALSO: Adaptation Etudes, Adapting to the Stage Etudes, Blackboard Workout, Cross-Cultural Etude, Filling-in-the-Front, Film Game, Film Reversal, Flashbacks and Flashforwards, Notecard Shuffle, Other Era, and Other Forms.

8

CHAPTER

Collaboration Etudes

THIS CHAPTER AND THE NEXT CONTAIN ETUDES INTENDED TO expand the reach and range of the playwright. Chapter 8 asks you to challenge your craft and creative impulses through collaborative efforts. Its purpose is to get you to interact with another playwright or artist—anyone, in fact, who is willing to play. You will try to find ways of stimulating your work toward new directions and new choices and away from habitual modes.

The primary goal of this series of collaboration etudes is to create a challenging situation in which partners can provide a stimulus for each other. The results will vary according to the partners, the risks being taken, the honesty of the reactions, and so on but should provide you with ways of reexamining your normal approaches and thinking methods. Second, although these exercises are not intended as a method of working collaboratively on a play, they could be very helpful toward that goal, especially in the sense of establishing the working rapport and open communication levels so essential to a successful project.

The primary purpose, however, is to provide a way of working that is more social than normal for a writer and that offers a set of obstacles a person might not provide for herself ordinarily. My other hope is that these exercises could also provide a foundation for establishing a workshop environment.

Workshops can be extraordinarily valuable environments for creative work, but they have their pitfalls as well. Many fail because they stop being about process and get turned into play-reading groups that focus too much on product. Acting and directing workshops and classes don't normally deal with presenting an entire work—why should playwrights? A workshop that can survive continues to deal with stimulating creative impulses and the development of craft skills. At any rate, the workshop environment can be a fertile ground. I urge writers to seek out one that will work for them, even if they must create their own.

Your approach to the etudes in this chapter will help you find out fairly quickly if you can work collaboratively. If it's not working for you after trying different combinations, so be it. This may not be the time for such work or you may not be a writer who can work with anyone else. There's no emphasis here on the idea of working together for the sole purpose of creating product. The main concept is seeking out other kinds of responses and stimuli for your own work process and craft development. You may feel stuck in your work or that the other etudes are no longer challenging you. You may want the presence of another person to create a yardstick to measure your responses to the exercises. Then again, you may not like or need any of this, and that's perfectly OK. As with all the etudes in this book, the underlying spirit is an unpressured, creative environment, not theatre boot camp.

I strongly recommend that you seek out a variety of people to work with, especially people from other disciplines. There are so many things to be learned from other art forms like painting and dance and from other kinds of work like accounting and the law. You could easily spend a lifetime working through the combinations. I know one of my own flaws is to seek out like-minded people in terms of world view, and politics, and I would encourage you to avoid that pitfall. What you can discover from working with people of differing values and backgrounds will be endlessly useful to you and to them.

Another pitfall to avoid is viewing collaboration as competitive game playing. It's easy to fall into one-upsmanship in such a situation. I've tried to suggest ways of playing such games with ground rules that should keep the competitive aspect in check, but I strongly suggest that you and your partner agree in advance on the point of your efforts. It would probably be a good idea as well to agree ahead on how to evaluate those efforts to establish some parameters for each other's feelings and needs.

Lastly, since it's possible that you might be the only playwright in town, however grim a thought that might be, I have suggested means of making these collaborations work on your own. They're less fun this way, but at least they can be accessed. If you are the only playwright in town and you don't plan to move, these collaboration etudes could be done pretty easily by fax or e-mail. People looking to network might try to do so through the Dramatists Guild as a starting point—simply announce your need for long-distance collaborators in the monthly *Newsletter* and see who responds.

You'll find that the etudes in this chapter and Chapter 9 do not have cross-reference sections. You and your partner will be able to discover other (and perhaps better) collaborative possibilities on your own after working through the etudes here. Further, I suggest that both of you should have tried most if not all of the etudes in the preceding chapters in order to have a solid craft grounding before attempting to work with another person's creative energies.

KEY ETUDES
Character **Collaboration**

Although this particular etude begins as the key, the first three etudes (Character, Plot, and Ground Plan collaborations) really form the heart of this chapter. I would suggest that you and a given partner work through all three before moving on to the others.

As with all key etudes, the purpose is to establish some fundamental ground rules and working concepts. The assumption in this chapter is that you will work with one or more collaborator(s) by swapping the given etude assignment, doing the etude, and then getting together to compare results and analyze the process. The analysis should be done in an open and constructive manner and might include such elements as how challenging the etude was (or wasn't), what kind of assets the collaborator's input added (or what challenges it created), what each collaborator felt about her own work on the etude, and whether an etude should be attempted again for reevaluation. Keep in mind that this is like spring training or early rehearsals—the point is to work on the rudiments of your own craft while creating a basic working relationship on which to build. Do not be hypercritical of yourself or your partner! Once you've evolved the basics of your working methods, the direction of the relationship will probably start to reveal itself. You may have found your Gilbert or Sullivan, an occasional playmate, or your Mr. or Ms. Hyde.

This first etude focuses on character for the very reason that the exercise will reveal the character of the collaborators through the characters you create. Questions will be raised in the process. Does this partner work creatively with the givens of the etude? Does this partner have a narrow or broad concept of character? Are you and your partner speaking the same essential language? As you encounter these and other questions, your feelings toward the answers will help you further define not only your collaborator but yourself as a partner as well. Do you demand too much or too little? Are you working broadly or narrowly? As already suggested, it may be that collaboration is not for you at all, and that's an acceptable conclusion to this effort. The main idea is to learn.

The Etude
Write a scene or monologue based on one or more character description(s) provided by your collaborator as she does the same. The description(s) provided should give clear indications of physical qualities and specify other characteristics without forcing the characterization toward certain kinds of behavior. Saying "this man murders when the moon is full" is not helpful; saying "this man has a homicidal streak in him somewhere" is a lot more open for your partner to react to and create from.

The purpose of this exercise is to challenge yourself to flesh out a character you probably would not have thought of on your own. It is also a psychological exploration of sorts since part of the exercise lends itself to speculating on why your partner created such a character and why you reacted to the character as you did. Everyone should avoid stereotypes in this etude unless there is a preplanned desire to examine stereotypes as a focal point.

Next, discuss the process and results with your partner and/or extend the exercise. Stick to analyzing your own work at first until the collaboration has reached a point at which commentary won't be threatening. It will help if you predetermine criteria for analysis, but don't be afraid to depart from this list in order to examine other aspects that present themselves. Lastly, don't treat the analytical part as psychotherapy; your partner probably doesn't want to know that the dead puppy of your childhood created an inability to write father characters with hats—save that aspect for somebody licensed to deal with it. This kind of etude work cannot and must not be a substitute for other needed kinds of work and self-help.

The etude can be extended in a variety of ways, most of which have to do with complicating the exercise you've already done. Try adding more characters, a character who radically affects the previous flow of the scene (e.g., introducing Godzilla into a scene about two women discussing their difficult relationships), a character who has a secret agenda, and so on. At this point you can also incorporate many of the other etudes in the book to help vary the work of this one.

You can do this etude on your own by gathering character descriptions from plays you haven't read or from character summaries in books of monologues or scenes for actors, or by using character breakdowns commonly provided in casting trade papers (such as *Backstage* in New York) and listed on bulletin boards in theatres. The fun of this exercise is that it asks you to recreate a character who already exists in another work. The difficulty is that you'll be working on characters who have already been created. In other words, the descriptions are the summary of a result rather than from an intuitive and undeveloped conjuring, which is what you should get in the partnered etude above.

Once you've selected a description to work from, write the piece and then see how yours compares to the original by reading or seeing the play from which the description was taken. Accepting that the differences will be very great because you didn't know the plot intended for the character, you can still do an analysis of your own work. What were your intuitive responses to the character description? What can you discover from the other playwright's choices for that same character? Don't get trapped into worrying about whose is better or worse, but try to examine the differences in the choice of language and sense of objective to get a stronger sense of the nature of those choices.

In all attempts at "self-collaboration," remember that the results are likely to be limited. It's kind of hard to sneak up on yourself, and you should treat this as a temporary situation while you search for ways of obtaining an actual collaborator. Nevertheless, the benefits of trying to reach outside your normal ways of working and thinking will always be worth the effort.

Finally, keep in mind that your possibilities for sources are innumerable and really only limited by yourself. Character descriptions from novels, the use of images from photos and paintings, and the descriptions of people from history of whom we have no recorded image (I remain intrigued by the memory of one theatre historian's description of Euripides as a redhead), and many more sources can provoke all kinds of responses in your writing. The world is your playground.

Plot Collaboration

There are variations on this etude further on in the chapter in Filling-in-the-Front, Rewrite, and Enhancement. This basic etude, along with the key etude (Character) and Ground Plan, is the foundation for the later exercises and for most of the others in the chapter. Remember these first three etudes should be tried before moving on.

The Etude

Each partner will come up with the first portion of a plot. This could be a single sentence, a few paragraphs, or the first pages of a script—the collaborators need to settle this point first. Once the beginning is created, the partners will swap and complete the portions in whatever manner has been previously agreed upon. Of course, I would urge that the response be done in a dramatized fashion rather than in a narrative one, but the manner must suit the needs and ambitions of the collaborators above any other agendas.

The key ground rule for this particular exercise is staying consistent with the given elements: If somebody is from Wales in the starting portion, they need to remain Welsh or you'll need to justify in changing them the fact that they were only pretending to be (or whatever). The learning will come from working within the discipline of what's given and of remaining faithful to another's concept. This work leads not only to good craft grounding but could even help you in other writing efforts—many writing jobs outside the theatre are assignments, after all ("Go write an article on pimple creams" or "You'll be writing episode 1,945 of *Life's Little Bubbles* next week, in which Delilah discovers that her lover was really her. . .").

The other basic ground rule is to avoid cornering your partner with a plot beginning that totally predicts the rest of the world. A more creative starting point might be to agree to trap each other in a murder mystery context with a very difficult solution. The locked-door type of mystery is the trickiest of this sort of plot: people are gathered in a closed room for some reason. Suddenly the lights go out. When they come on, somebody's dead. Who done it? I once had a role in a locked-door mystery play called *The Thirteenth Chair* written in 1916 by Bayard Veiller (Samuel French, Inc.) that had an ingenious solution. There are a great many others to use as models, and the murder mystery plot gives you lots of room for ingenious plot games.

Sources for this version of the Plot Collaboration etude might come from real-life crime stories and from the kind of weird-but-true stories found in such collections as *The People's Almanac* or *Learned Pigs and Fireproof Women* by Ricky Jay, the daily newspaper, or any other sources you can discover on your own. I should hasten to add, however, that crime or weird-but-true stories are not the only possibilities; partners should spend some time on what kinds of stories intrigue them most and develop some working models from that exploration.

There are any number of variations on this basic etude. The partners could agree to write alternate points in an outline of a plot and then work on scenes for the points written by the other. They could agree to watch the first ten minutes of an unknown film or TV show and write their own versions of how the plot would follow from that beginning. I would highly recommend mining the etudes from Chapter 6 for other alternatives.

A writer working on this etude alone could start from reading an unfamiliar play and stopping after ten pages to finish the plot—in which case, you're now drifting into the realm of copying a given style and adding a different dimension to your work (see Style Copy in Chapter 7). You could use an unfamiliar film or TV show to do the same. Certainly reading the first chapter of a novel would be a challenging way to approach this, as would asking a friend to tell you the beginning of a personal story. Of course, the point is to find a starting stimulus to work from and then complete that process with careful analysis.

Ground Plan Collaboration

This etude is a favorite with classes and has no limit to the variations you can try. I find it particularly helpful because I'm not immediately visual in my own work; having to deal with a physical reality asks me to commit to that sense from the beginning.

As you will note quickly, the nature of this etude is such that you probably need to have worked on the character and plot collaborations before trying Ground Plan just to be sure your communications are open and flowing. It's possible that you and your collaborator are far more visual in approach than I am and you may not have needed these other steps. (It's also important to keep in mind that if a given etude seems like a complete flop, it may be that you needed to proceed in a slow fashion. Don't quit until you've looked at a multitude of possibilities.)

The Etude

Write a scene or monologue based on a ground plan, set design, or set description provided by a partner. It's important that the design not be so manipulated that you are forced into choices unless you agree in advance with your partner. The place needs to be specific but not too specific. The essence of the choice is to come up with a place that is provocative and dramatic.

One aspect of this etude is to challenge yourself when writing the scene to make the space come alive so that your characters have a genuine stake in the environment. Utilize the unique characteristics of the place (it's a house on stilts or used to be a monastery).

The other challenge is to use as many of the elements of the space as actively as possible. As a ground rule, try to use everything in the space in a way that is crucial both to the action and the meaning of the scene. A den filled with collected weapons is highly suggestive, but what of? It's one thing to have all your characters arm themselves from the walls and fight, it's another if one character is using the fact of the weapons being there to intimidate another. Both approaches take advantage of the same weaponry and potentiality, but for different uses. Not every space is so evocative of course, but the point here is to make your setting evocative. You can dramatize even the most mundane space. A room with one window and one chair can become extremely charged.

Naturally, part of the analysis of this etude will be how the dramatization matches the space described. You should also compare the dramatic use of this space to your normal employment of space in plays. For instance, do you make a concerted effort to choose elements in your plays' spaces that will be theatrical and meaningful? Or do you assume that this is the designer's job? Are you accustomed to writing strictly for naturalistic or surreal environments? Make an arrangement with your partner to suggest spaces that will take you out of the customary so you can explore your potential. You could also look for a partner whose style is so different from your own that this person's customary conceptualization of theatrical space will do the same thing. Seeking out a set designer, painter, or other visual artist would be fun for this kind of exercise (take a look at the Other Forms etude).

If you have no partner available, tap another source such as the ground plan from a play you don't know, finding illustrations of sets or real places from magazines or books, or even reading narrative descriptions of sets or places. If you're working from the ground plan of an unfamiliar play, your analysis would be similar to that of the Character Collaboration. See how your scene is both different and similar in comparison to the source.

You can also create a scene based on limiting elements of a given ground plan (or illustration or description) rather than trying to be all-inclusive. In this instance, the point would be to impose an extreme selectivity, in effect redesigning the design through the writing. For example, if your partner gave you a painter's studio with an iron chandelier in the ceiling, you might choose to ignore all but the chandelier and focus only on that element. In another approach, you might eliminate the chandelier and select only the paint-splattered floor as a primary element.

An extension would be to write varying perspectives on the space based on who is populating that space. In a bar, for instance, you might write from the perspective of the bartender's disgust with drunks, a disgust embodied in the way the bartender relates to the bottles and the bar itself. Another scene might be from the perspective of a person whose relationship has ended in the bar, so that a particular table would take on the metaphorical weight of the breakup. But the same table might represent to another couple the beginning of their successful relationship. It would be fun to have the characters of a given scene talk about the space itself so that you could examine the space through the characters' values and sense of the space.

OTHER ETUDES
Dialogue Collaboration
This is a wonderful etude for developing trust with your partner and for focusing on concentration. It should be done over and over and might even serve as an excellent warmup for your work sessions. As a technical enhancement, this etude is a fun way of putting some muscle into your own dialogue because the challenge is to respond to someone else's writing, which makes the process wholly unpredictable. Anything we can do to challenge our habits and reexamine our thought processes is vital to continued growth.

The Etude
Working with your partner, develop a piece over several pages with each person writing one line of dialogue only. A "line" can be one word or a paragraph, but a line is the entire statement or response of one character. As always, less is more. I would suggest that you start with a two-character scene and experiment with this collaboration a number of times before taking on more characters. In this first version each partner is responsible for one character throughout; when you go to more than two characters you'll need to develop some ground rules concerning responsibilities.

The object of this etude is to open your responses to where your partner is taking the scene while keeping an integrity about the character(s) you're writing. I have found this exercise can develop quickly into a very entertaining seesaw battle: there is a tension that exists almost instantly because your character has no way of knowing what the other character will say or do, unlike the normal playwriting circumstance when you are the voice of both. This situation adds several demands. First, you must try to be as clear in your character as you can be (unless your purpose is to be otherwise, which is valid but can be very wearing). Second, you must focus on motivating both the active and reactive elements of your character (sometimes the character may be stuck with merely answering, but the answer must still be an active part of the character's objectives and agenda). Lastly, both writers must keep the scene as organic as possible.

Keeping everything organic refers to maintaining the integrity of the script, not imposing rules arbitrarily, and not tossing out elements willy-nilly. An organic spirit is not only a crucial concept for this etude but for playwriting in general: if your character introduces an idea or a physical element into the scene, don't just allow it to get dropped. Plan a use for the element; even if your character cannot actually get to the use, that character should actively try. Well-trained actors, for example, are taught to follow through on any action until they can no longer do so, which leads them to the next action: if your character says she's leaving, then she should keep on going until something or someone in the scene forces her to stop. Whatever stops the leaving is the start of the next series of actions, all of which should be followed out to the fullest as well.

A simple but crucial variation would be agreeing to write every other sentence in a given scene so that you're no longer responsible only for character A but are now writing for both. This variation involves agreeing beforehand that each character will say more than one sentence in a given line as often as possible.

A much more difficult version is built on agreeing to write every other word, an exercise that requires enormous concentration in order to continue making sense. This exercise can lead to some choices of language that will be rather wonderful—if you only have one word by which to direct or continue a beat, your word choices will become much more careful and clever. It also means that sometimes you'll be stuck with less-wonderful choices where the sense of the sentence puts you at the only logical word that must come next, usually a preposition. Don't forget that punctuation can enter into your consideration, however. Where an *of* might seem to be the only choice, a dash followed by a new word—*however*, for instance—might give you more room to play.

A still more difficult variation is having each partner write a monologue. This must be active so the character is seeking something strongly dramatic (no "I remember" or "the sunset tonight is like my heart" kind of stuff). Swap your monologues and then proceed to build a scene from your partner's work. This might be a scene that begins with the monologue, builds to it, springs out of an idea in the monologue without actually using the speech, and so on.

A more challenging variation is to use only dialogue from the monologue for character A while you create the dialogue for character B to respond to these selected lines from A to move the scene along. At the same time, your partner will be creating dialogue to work with the monologue you wrote. It's a little like taking scissors to a narrative, a la William S. Burroughs, to restructure the dialogue, but the point here is to discover what possibilities lie within the monologue.

As with other etudes, the Dialogue Collaboration has a relationship to an acting exercise often done by directors in which the director speaks out the questions that lead to the each part of a monologue to help the actor find motivation for each line and beat. For instance, with the actor saying "To be," the director might say, "What's the alternative?" Actor: "Or not to be. That is the question." Director: "Oh, really? How did it get to be the question?" Actor: "Whether 'tis nobler to . . ." This exercise reminds an actor that all the words said in a play, even in a monologue, are in dramatic reaction to an action. The idea is to get the actor to think of the monologue as a dramatic reaction to an internal struggle (with the side coach providing the germs of the struggle) rather than just saying a whole lot of words without interruption.

Working alone on this etude is trickier than for other collaborations. The best method I can think of would be playing games used for improvisational acting. One such game involves writing down a variety of lines on pieces of paper, drawing the lines from a hat, and then trying to fashion a somewhat coherent scene in response to these random lines. Again, a major element of this particular etude is reacting to the unplanned while trying to actively move forward in the scene at the same time, so the lines in the hat shouldn't be too difficult to respond to. In fact, you might salt the pile with lines that simply say "Yes" or "No" or ask a question such as "What do you mean?" just to give yourself a break.

In another game, you also write lines and put them into a hat, but the first line you draw becomes the first line of your scene and the second line you draw becomes the last. You then write a scene to fill in between the two. A further variation involves copying a page of a script, cutting out lines from it, and drawing those lines from a hat—the difference being that the lines would no longer be of your own creation. A final option for this would be to begin from the Found Situations etude as a starting point. Record an overheard conversation as faithfully as possible, then write dialogue to fill in the gaps and theatricalize the found words.

A last suggestion would be to collaborate by electronic means. A telephone, fax, or e-mail could be other sources to respond to; keep in mind that you mustn't be so literal about your collaborator that you only seek out another playwright or artist. Remember that your purpose in any of this work is to increase your capabilities as a dramatic writer, so any stimulus will do.

Enhancement

This etude is based on the concept of taking something to the next level of impact and meaning. It is an exercise in adding rather than taking away. The key to the success of this collaboration is a clear understanding of the nature of what is to be added.

Keep in mind that this etude is about enhancement rather than "improvement"—don't take the attitude that you're going to make your partner's scene "better." Fulfill the exercise in the spirit of its ground rule: experiment with the effect of adding elements to a scene.

The Etude

Begin by having partner A write a scene or sketch of everyday behavior. This scene should be written to be as naturalistic as possible and it could even be based on a found situation (see the Found

Situations etude). The scene should be kept as simple as possible without completely sacrificing dramatic quality. The piece could be something from an existing play of partner A so long as that partner is willing to have the scene played with. The next step is for partner B to rewrite the scene by adding various elements to affect the impact and/or meaning of the scene.

The first addition would be to relocate the scene to enhance the meaning of the dialogue. For example, a scene written originally about two guys discussing the merits of various cars would be enhanced by relocating it to the Daytona 500. The scene would be focused on something more immediate and could be affected by the intrusion of the locale into the scene (e.g., screaming fans or a crash). The same dialogue would be changed quite radically if spoken by two guys getting ready to defend a foxhole against an assault.

Another enhancement would be the addition of set, prop, or costume elements. The introduction of a weirdly humming toy into a kitchen or the armband of some extremist group on one character could change the scene.

The last enhancement would be to add behavior to alter the feeling or meaning of a scene, such as giving one character a terrible stammer or having another character become touchy-feely. The next step from any of these would be to give the enhanced scene or sketch back to the original writer and ask her to respond to the enhancement by rewriting the piece.

As in several of the other collaborations, the basis for this etude is reacting to the unexpected and uncontrolled. Having your suburban strip mall scene relocated to a space station has got to challenge you to think beyond your normal next step. The overall enhancement this collaboration can provide is to move the scene to a more metaphorical level. Choices of locale, set, and behavior can all increase the symbolic power of a given piece of writing—provided they're good choices, of course. The issue then becomes the nature of those choices. What does a Nazi armband say beyond the dialogue?

My personal standard for theatre is that everything that happens onstage has to carry at least a double load: the story and the meaning of the story. An exercise like this etude is designed to get at the second aspect of that load. In swapping the material back and forth, part of the process will be discovering the kinds of meaning your partner endows your work with. The possible variations are limitless; repeat this etude as often as you like or need to keep mining the possibilities.

A way of generating new ideas on your own would be to enhance a scene from a published play or from an existing scene of your own. Choosing a scene from something written a long while back might be simplest, but making the enhancement really radical or silly could also give you some necessary distance. It's harder to challenge your own work of course, but pushing yourself to extremes can result in some very interesting discoveries.

Exposition

In this collaboration, you work from a given fact about a character. The partners should do the Character Collaboration first before attempting this exercise to work on basic characterization and/or to create a character for this particular collaboration.

The Etude

Partner A creates a fact about a chosen character that partner B then has to reveal in an indirect way as part of a scene. These terms mean that the character cannot announce her fact; the playwright must find a way of implying the information in a way that is integral to the action of the scene. The fact about the character may be something difficult, like a secret, or just some background aspect which is important to fleshing out the personality, like being a computer whiz or keeping bees as a hobby. The scene should be written as a stand-alone piece with its own objectives and actions and not as a scene that is only about getting out this bit of exposition.

The discussion following the etude should be about the success of revealing the exposition but could also include some exchange on how to improve anything that might not have been entirely successful. This postmortem should include your viewpoints about exposition as an element of plays—assuming you haven't already discussed them prior to the exercise. Some people believe that a play should happen completely in a present that requires no exposition because a character's past is irrelevant. Others ascribe to other concepts.

A promising variation on this etude would be providing a different kind of exposition, such as a character being caught in a lie about something. The point might become writing the scene expressly for the purpose of dealing with the impact of the exposition once revealed—the scene would then be about the exposition.

This collaboration can be converted more easily than others to a solo etude since you can make up any fact for yourself to reveal in a scene that you wish and the essential challenge will still be there. Take a look at the Secret Behavior, Secret Objective, and Secret Past etudes in earlier chapters. An alternative would be to borrow exposition from other sources. Take the very first expositional fact provided in any form you select (e.g., a mention of someone's history in a novel or a fact in a magazine article) and write that into a scene.

Extended Dialogue

This etude is a more complex version of the Dialogue Collaboration. I would suggest very strongly that both partners do that exercise before attempting this one.

The Etude

Each partner starts a sketch with two characters and writes ten to fifteen lines of the sketch—there should be agreed-upon limits set before beginning. Each partner then turns her sketch over to the other writer to continue for the next limit of lines. The object is for each to continue the swapped sketch in the same style, set of objectives, and character qualities as begun by the other. You should also keep the same elements intact (such as not just ignoring the introduction of a box of candy in the other's lines).

The obvious difference from the Dialogue Collaboration is that this exercise has more to struggle with and work from than the other; the input is much greater on each side, and many of the terms are already set before the second partner gets the material. Be careful to avoid manipulation in this collaboration. The temptation might be to write something that you know the other will not be able to alter easily or to write something that the other might feel hampered from responding to (such as writing something blatantly racist or gross with a partner who is extremely sensitized to such things). The analysis afterwards should take into consideration the greater difficulty of this as compared to the Dialogue Collaboration.

One variation on this basic exercise might be having more than two characters. The challenge here is keeping all the characters balanced in their participation in the scene. It would be easy just to include a person who periodically mutters something incoherent in a bar scene; it would be far more difficult to collaboratively craft a scene in which three characters are actively struggling toward strong objectives.

Working solo on this etude would be best done with short fragments of plays you don't already know, with the obvious limitation being that you can only work from them as opposed to having the fragment continue from your work. Again, it seems that electronic collaboration is the best answer to being without a partner in your immediate environment.

Filling-in-the-Front
This etude is more of a game than the other collaborations because it is based on a built-in challenge.

The Etude
Partner A writes the end of a scene. This end might be just the very last line or it may be a sequence of some length; you will need to predetermine the terms, of course. The job of partner B is to write the scene(s) that will organically lead to this end.

The partners might want to predetermine how long a preceding scene can be or impose a time limit on the writing to add an additional level of difficulty to the process.

Keep in mind as well that there may be a variety of ways to get to the end that partner A creates. For instance, an ending in which someone says an emotional farewell and then jumps from a building ledge is either the tragic finale of a serious suicide threat or the ludicrous result of a preceding scene that establishes that the ledge is three feet high. This collaboration asks you to go toward the given end in a linear fashion or to bend what precedes the end to a non-linear shape. It would be very useful to try several different filling-in-the-front approaches to the same ending just to help you extend yourself beyond your immediate solution to the ending and nudge you out of your normal patterns. As in the Extended Dialogue etude, I think this exercise will be more effective if the partners have tried earlier etudes in this chapter first.

For a partnerless approach, pick an unknown play at random and use the last page of the play as the ending toward which to write. Make comparisons with the source and your own exercise for analysis—they're bound to be quite different. What can you discover about the other's thinking processes and your own that will deepen your understanding of how your work evolves?

Rewrite

This collaboration is more corrective in nature than any of the others. It is riskier on one hand, but the exercise offers many potential insights into each other's writing styles and values. Trust between the partners is essential.

The Etude

Begin with each partner writing a sketch from beginning to end. Set a length restriction beforehand (I would suggest three to five pages as a starting point). This sketch should be written in a single sitting and within a predetermined time limit. Once completed, the other partner rewrites the sketch. This rewrite should be approached in specific ways, however, or the results will be chaotic.

The first step would be to go through and excise anything that is perceived by the "rewriter" to be extraneous: any dialogue, action, or set elements. The second step would be to look carefully through the script for any moments of dialogue that might be replaced or enhanced by behavior. The third step would be to look at the script as to its beginning and end to see whether it could be improved by pruning away any unnecessary preamble or resolution. (This idea is based on the concept of "get in late, get out early." See the etude by the same title for a further discussion of this concept.)

Once the rewriter has finished, return the piece to the originator. After absorbing the rewrite, a discussion between the partners should ensue. The object of this discussion is why various choices were made. Partner A might be a bit sensitive about partner B's cuts and changes, but a conversation about the basis for these choices is likely to lead to discoveries about craft and craft values. Keep in mind that what's being discussed in this etude is merely a sketch, after all, so there's not very much at stake.

Of course, any play is a highly subjective organism and created by a wide set of factors within the individual writer, but we can all benefit from having someone else help us discover the muscle in our work. Trimming away excess, getting to the dramatic point, and keeping an eye on the "show, don't tell" ideal for our work can only result in better scripts, though remember that I'm talking exclusively in regard to the exercise. While it's helpful to learn how to be open to comments and questions about our material when we do readings and workshops, there's a line that must always be observed about avoiding comments that literally tell someone what or how to write.

Finally, listening to another's perspective tells us a good deal more about our own perspective. If you find yourself constantly defending your choices, maybe it's time to shut up and just listen. Perhaps the other person's point of view isn't right for your particular work, but then again maybe your haste to defend your choices isn't right either.

One way of trying this etude on your own is rewriting someone's published play—as an exercise only of course, since you don't want to violate someone's copyright. This exercise can help you to understand the nature of someone else's choices and the qualities of a particular era or style. A further variation would be to take a play from the past, rewrite the language into modern speech, and then apply the cutting and substitution concepts of this etude as well. This approach verges on adaptation, so you might want to go back and take another look at the Adaptation etudes as well.

Yet another variation would be writing a sketch on your own, letting it sit for a week, then coming back and taking the same series of steps described above. Treat your sketch as if it were written by someone else and see what you can discover through the rewrite process. We hear about professional baseball pitchers revitalizing their careers by developing a new pitch, but we don't often think about the pitches we choose to use as writers. Your style and individualized expression are crucial, but have they also become self-limiting?

Swap

This is probably a silly name for this etude, but I wanted to place it last alphabetically and it's the best I could come up with. The idea behind the etude is anything but silly, however, which is why it's last. For some this concept may seem completely radical, and that's why it's an idea well worth your consideration. As with all the etudes, the underlying philosophy is grounded in having a willingness to fail by attempting to extend one's reach. If we remain safe in our playwriting methods, we can become incapable of achieving new expressiveness or perspectives.

The Etude

Seek out artists from other media and disciplines and then look for ways to "swap" art between you as source material for projects as well as swapping impressions of each other's work. In the second instance, the idea is to have someone paint a reaction to a piece you've written, and you would write a piece based on a different work of hers. In both cases you're looking for ways of reseeing your own work through the aesthetics and processes of another.

By working on the ideas generated by someone's painting or piece of music, you open your creative channels. It's particularly intriguing to work with an artist and to have the opportunity to see and talk about that person's work. The commonalities and differences can be extremely revealing about thought processes, intuition, and creative pitfalls and demons. If it's possible, arrange to see that person at work. What you will see in terms of concentration, use of the body, and relationship with that particular "instrument" (piano, paint brush, or body) will be highly informative. And while it may seem pretty dull for someone to watch a writer, it can be very instructive to people from other forms, so don't be afraid to swap in this respect as well.

Seeing how another artist reacts to your material will be very informative for you. It's been my experience that a storyteller, choreographer, or musician will first adapt your story into a form more workable for their own medium, and then move into various levels of interpretation, metaphorization, and so on. In time, you will see your creation reinterpreted through this other work, and this mirror can be a fascinating way of reperceiving your own.

This etude can be of particular value if you're feeling lost in your piece. Having someone feed your material back to you in a creative way is very liberating because this person is not imposing the same kind of pressures on you that a director and cast might be inclined to. The reason you may be lost isn't necessarily because the piece doesn't work—it may be simply that you've lost your sense of the original image or idea that captured your imagination and set the piece in motion. Other artists tend to go to the heart of your work and often reveal to us what that heart is when we've long since lost sight of it.

I also find dealing with other artistic disciplines refreshing because inevitably the discussion focuses on the challenges and frustrations of the form. If you stop at this moment of reading and consider that at this very instant there are thousands of artists in every conceivable medium who are working on something new and coping with the challenges that new work is presenting—stop here for a minute—then you'll have, I hope, a reassurance that you're not struggling alone in your craft. At every moment of every day, artists are reinventing a medium and themselves to carry their visions forward. Keeping that notion in mind as you work can help take away some loneliness and shrink the mountain by at least a few feet.

If you're lucky enough to be multitalented, you can attempt this etude alone, although it will be far less satisfying. Respond to your own work in another medium in which you have some ability. Even if you're not a trained photographer, for instance, you could go out with your point-and-shoot camera and try to collect images that resonate with your piece in some way. Or do stick-figure drawings. It's irrelevant as to whether the response is great art or not; the issue is always going to be finding new perspective from other approaches and media.

9

CHAPTER

Unblocking Etudes

I WAS ONCE SO PLAGUED BY WRITER'S BLOCK THAT I COULDN'T even write a letter. One morning I was on my way out to meet my friend Bruce (who was always willing to listen to my sob stories) for a late breakfast and, I hoped, some advice to relieve this monster block. I decided to check the mail first, however. In my box was a letter with a Washington, D.C., return address, and I thought, Great, I'm being audited. I opened the envelope. The letter inside said, "Dear Mr. Wright, This is to notify you that you have received a National Endowment for the Arts Playwright Fellowship." Needless to say, breakfast with my friend turned into a celebration instead of a whine-session, and my writer's block magically went away. I was validated.

Since that time I have never experienced anything more than minor blocks, but I know others who have suffered terribly, so I've developed the etudes in this chapter to address the problem.

I hasten to say that writer's block is going to affect people at various levels. In other words, your block may be complex or it may be a simple lack of confidence. These etudes should not be regarded as cures, but ways of trying to write through a block. If playing with these etudes doesn't help, I'd suggest talking with other artists, or going into therapy. Above all: don't suffer. We are creative spirits, and in making our art, we sometimes tap into places inside ourselves we've never touched before or have hidden away. Sometimes those parts of ourselves declare themselves off-limits and so shut down the thing that accessed them. Therapy, advice from friends, and these etudes are all ways of working on the problem rather than being paralyzed by it.

The etudes that follow are playful attempts to address your block from a sort of "get back on the horse" kind of perspective. While you figure out where the block came from (if you ever do), you are still writing. Keeping that single fact in mind can do wonders, in fact, because you can say to yourself "I am still writing. I may not be writing my own personal definition of a masterpiece, but I am still writing."

On that note, I would be remiss if I didn't suggest that this entire book could be useful for dealing with writer's block. Going through each chapter or picking out exercises at random would be solid means of getting back in the writing groove. The etudes in this chapter are simply more dedicated to the writer's block dilemma. In all cases, the process is about working and thinking theatrically and keeping the channels open.

A final note: the etudes in this chapter are not cross-referenced as in the first seven chapters. There are some suggestions made here and there, but my primary intention is for you to work on these etudes and then seek out others on your own. By following your own intuition about what additional etudes to play with, you will very likely be telling yourself where your concerns and problems are. Trust your choices and see where they lead you.

KEY ETUDE
They're Talking About You
This etude's approach is designed to give you a perspective on yourself from other points of view. There are several variations contained within the etude itself.

The Etude
Create a scene in which the characters are talking about your block. Let them have as much fun with it or take it as seriously as you like, but do everything you can to keep it honest and up front. Try to avoid characters who pity you or who excessively trash you unless you really feel the need for some masochism. Let the characters do the talking and don't try to manipulate the material.

I would suggest starting with arbitrarily made-up characters. If no one comes to mind, work from the personalities of people you know. Pick people at first who will be sympathetic (without overdoing it) but who don't psychoanalyze you. Allow these characters to discuss you, your block, how you look today, what the weather's like, and so on. Avoid analysis of any kind at all cost. The point is to write about your writing problem, not to treat yourself as an experimental lab animal or political prisoner.

From this beginning you might want to try some basic variations: have the same characters discuss you before the block started; have them discuss your block as if it's over. Use characters based on your best friends and your worst enemies. Find characters based on people you knew in childhood. Draw especially from people you know whose evaluations of your work may have stymied you. For a time I always rewrote certain lines because I could picture a particular friend standing behind me going "tsk, tsk, tsk" as I wrote. It took a lot for me to stop worrying about this friend's judgment, but my work became more fluid, free, and organic to my personality when I did. My friend's dramaturgy wasn't at fault, but my preworrying about meeting his expectations was.

To try something more whimsical, use famous or mythical characters—Hamlet, Auntie Mame, or Sisyphus—as the people discussing your work. Do anything that will allow you to be fanciful and to have some fun with this etude. Don't be afraid to let the characters from the play you've been working on talk. Be willing to try any number of variations.

OTHER ETUDES
Games
Although all the etudes in this book are games, the ones I'm going to discuss are game-specific in the sense that they have fun and easily obtainable goals involved. These games are taken from standard improvisational acting exercises and theatre games.

The perspective of this etude is somewhat different from the others in this chapter, which are more focused on dealing with your writer's block through writing. The idea with this etude is to write for the sake of writing, to have some fun in the process, and to treat yourself as someone recovering from a trauma of some kind (I hope that doesn't sound too dramatic). The "trauma" is the writer's block and the notion of the recovery here is to work your way back to health by taking small steps and doing easier things until you're ready to go back to the level before the block set in. Treat these etudes as walks or stretches for your recovering body.

The Etude

In order to provoke yourself to write in a manner in which the result is largely obtainable, play the following games with yourself to see what starts to emerge.

Alphabet Game

Starting from any place you wish in the alphabet, write a sequence of lines in which each subsequent line begins with the next letter of the alphabet:

CLIFF : Aren't you late?
OLIVE: Believe it.
CLIFF: Can't you just start earlier?
OLIVE: Don't "start" with me.

As you can readily see, the form invites compressed dialogue—one-line responses—and is fun to write.

Yes or No

Create a scene between two characters, one of whom can only answer yes or no to anything the other says. A simple variation would be to restrict the character to only no or only yes. You'll find that this game is very challenging and frustrating; it helps if the other character already knows the conditional nature of the yes or no character.

Mood/Genre Shift

Using one card for each, make a set of notecards that describe various moods or mental states (happy, sad, depressed, confused) or various entertainment genres (soap opera, porn film, musical, Western). Begin writing a scene for two people. If you can't think of anything, have them retell a fairy tale. At certain intervals—using a timer would be best—select a notecard and adjust the scene according to what's on the card. A scene between two people who are madly in love would shift in one way if you're playing Mood Shift and the card that comes up is "sad" and would shift in quite a different way if you're playing Genre Shift and the "musical" card comes up. A fun variation on this would be to play both at once by selecting a card or more from each. In this way you might end up with a "sad" "musical" "porn film." There are many potential variations here.

There are far too many etudes in the book to list as possible alternatives or additions to the games already mentioned. I would suggest that you look through the book again and pull out etudes with game potential such as Questions Only. Keep in mind that the spirit of playing is at the forefront here. Try not to pick etudes that have previously frustrated you. Remember, this etude emphasizes the idea of slowly returning to your former writer's strength.

Journal

Ben Herman, my first writing teacher, once asked me how my work was going. I told him I hadn't been writing much lately and how it was bothering me that my output was so puny. He then asked me if my eyes were OK. I told him yes. And my ears? Yes again. "Good, then you're still observing—the writing will come out of that." In Ben's view, we are writing all the time—putting pen to paper is just the last of a long and complicated series of actions.

The Etude

Keep a journal on your writing block. Be as detailed and analytical as you like since it's private. Incorporate as much detail of your day and where you're sitting at the time of writing and what you remember of your dreams and fantasies as possible. The point here is to let go of worrying about the block as if it's an immutable fact of life. As Ben helped me see, we're always recording, sifting, and reperceiving. A journal makes those facts present and realized.

If you're having such a problem that you can't put fingers to keyboard, or pen to paper, then get a tape recorder and talk your journal into it. Do anything you can to record your days and observations. In doing this, what you provide is a self-validation that reminds you of the ceaselessness of your creativity. You can't help it, after all; it's endemic to your very spirit. So what if there's no "product" at the moment? Rather than using those energies to fret over not writing, harness them to write about not writing and to continue consciously what you do every day unconsciously: observe, record, and recall.

As we well know, many writers keep journals. What perhaps doesn't get acknowledged is that they often keep various kinds of journals—perhaps a sort of permanent one for private comments, a portable one for jotting down observations or snippets of conversations, a more whimsical one for keeping visual records in (photos and clippings from magazines), and so on. The idea of this journal is to keep track of a particular journey you're taking—like a ship's diary—but there's no reason why you couldn't have other journals of daily or weekly writing going on. Do anything you need to in order to keep yourself busy writing, short of filling hundreds of books with "All work and no play make Jack a dull boy."

Other Forms

Typically, we trap ourselves into living and creating as if we're mounted on tracks from which we cannot depart. If you're fortunate enough to have abilities in other forms of expression, this etude should be a natural for you; if you don't think you possess those abilities, think again.

The Etude

Set out a daily time period when you can work without disturbance. In this time period, try to give other parts of yourself a voice in coming to terms with your block. For example, draw about it, write music about it, cook about it, garden about it. If you don't do any of these normally, try them. If you don't do any of them particularly well, try them anyway. Nobody says you have to draw up to some artistic standard; the point is to please yourself—a heartfelt doodle or tune in the right spirit equals a masterpiece any time.

One of my luckier discoveries was a love for photography. In my periods of uncertainty about my writing or about a project I was in the midst of, I found that wandering around with camera in hand was a wonderful way of addressing the problem. I wasn't writing per se, but I was putting my mind to a creative challenge: selecting something to photograph, deciding on an approach to this subject, trying variations on the approach, snapping the shot, getting the film developed (or doing it myself), and making the prints. All of these acts were a hands-on connection with my creative self— maybe not my writer self, but a good friend of my writer self.

Photography does not require thousands of dollars' worth of gear. I started with a point-and-shoot camera and often return to it, just to free myself from the imposition that technology can some- times become. The issue is seeing first of all, and the exploration beyond that is into what you choose to see and how. All creative efforts teach you to use your brain in different ways than you cus- tomarily do. I'd even go so far as to say that you should be doing this kind of exercise whether you have a block or not.

Other options would include making collages—taking existing images and reshaping them into different statements—or sewing or woodworking. A friend in New York used to amuse herself by paint- ing her chairs and radiators all kinds of vivid colors to enliven her home space and to rethink what furniture and decor were all about. Another friend spent hours putting together soundtracks for his lat- est play or idea to see what another artistic form would jog loose. Anything you can make into a creative project will do so long as you work on communicating with your block. When you allow the part of you that's blocked in one direction to go free in another, creation can continue or begin again.

A final suggestion in this area would be to consider adaptation as a way of freeing yourself. The Adaptation Etudes in Chapter 4 would be very helpful. Working from someone else's idea and story will challenge you to think about writing from a less worrisome place than dealing with your own ideas and approaches. There are other kinds of problems endemic to adaptation, but if you'll keep yourself away from a concern with product, these etudes should be excellent catalysts to get working again.

Short Forms

Another issue that seems to block people up is that they can't get their whole play, film, or novel to work so it must be no good. If the work is no good, then they must be no good.

Unless you're under some kind of deadline guillotine, why

drive yourself crazy trying to finish something that you've lost the handle on? Work in short forms instead for a while to see if the handle will return.

The Etude

Write a series of ten-minute plays about the subject of your unfinished-and-driving-you-crazy longer play. Or write a series of haiku, one-page short stories, or a book for five year olds. Certainly you could do any of the etudes in this entire book as ways of approaching your material in a short form manner by simply imposing a length restriction on yourself. None of these may solve the problem that you face with your piece, but they will permit you to move out of that paralyzed-at-the-keyboard place and into some other kind of writing.

My last comments on being blocked have to do with the tendency many of us have to keep on pushing at a given problem or situation as if the sheer rigor of our onslaught is itself a solution. I have learned through my own experiences and from those shared by friends that sometimes you need to just let go of a given difficulty and let it stew for a while.

When we try to "make it work" we're often just adding a new level of stress to an existing level of stress. My own personal advice is to take a day or a week off with the same kind of rigor with which you were just trying to pound your project into shape. Do not, in other words, feel guilty about taking a break.

Even if your writing is going smoothly, it's not a bad idea to give yourself a little space now and then. Go to a movie in the afternoon on a weekday just to name one kind of simple pleasure. Whatever idea you had won't vanish in the popcorn, and when you return to your work you may find that the outside stimulus has provided you with new energy for your efforts.

Many artists fear that if they stop working for an extended period or they try to retool their work methods they'll never be able to get back to where they were. This fear is largely a matter of habit and personal insecurity. History shows that the most creative individuals have often thrown off an old methodology or philosophy or even changed mediums altogether to find their greatest level of expression. Change for the sake of change is not necessarily going to lead us to new realms, but it can certainly raise important questions about the realm in which we've labored. We sometimes hesitate to ask ourselves these questions for fear of losing our security but we need to remember that one of many acceptable answers is "I like the way I've always worked." The point is asking; it is about challenging yourself. Writer's block is often an unasked (or unconsciously asked) question related in one way or another to whether one's work is valid or not. The answer will always be yes *because* you are questioning.

Writer's block is healthy at a certain level. It's our mind putting on the brakes and forcing us to take the time to reassess and reaffirm. Flowing with that need to take the time gives you much more room to make the best use of that time.

ALPHABETICAL LIST OF ETUDES

ALPHABETICAL LIST OF ETUDES

FOR FURTHER READING

The following is a selected list of plays and books I've referred to.

Archer, William. *From Ibsen's Workshop*
Beckett, Samuel. *End Game*
Blessing, Lee. *Eleemosynary*
Chekov, Anton. *The Three Sisters*
Churchill, Caryl. *Cloud Nine*
Engel, Lehman. *The Making of a Musical*
Fornes, Maria Irene. *The Conduct of Life, The Danube*
Friel, Brian. *The Faith Healer; Philadelphia, Here I Come*
Guare, John. *The House of Blue Leaves*
Hellman, Lillian. *The Little Foxes*
Ibsen, Henrik. *A Doll's House*
Inge, William. *Bus Stop*
Innaurato, Albert. *The Transfiguration of Benno Blimpie*
Johnstone, Keith. *Impro: Improvisation and the Theatre*
Kushner, Tony. *Angels in America, A Bright Room Called Day*
Lapine, James. *Twelve Dreams*
Mamet, David. *Edmond, Glengarry Glen Ross, On Directing Film*
Mann, Emily. *Execution of Justice, Still Life*
Margulies, Donald. *The Model Apartment*
Meyers, Patrick. *K–2*
Miller, Arthur. *A View from the Bridge, After the Fall, All My Sons, Death of a Salesman*

FOR FURTHER READING

Moliere. *Tartuffe*, *The Misanthrope*

Muller, Heiner. *Hamletmachine*

Norman, Marsha. *Getting Out*, *'Night Mother*, *Trudy Blue*

O'Neill, Eugene. *Strange Interlude*

Overmyer, Eric. *In a Pig's Valise*

The Performance Group. *Dionysus in 69*

Pinter, Harold. *Betrayal*

Shaffer, Anthony. *Sleuth*

Shaffer, Peter. *Amadeus*, *Equus*

Shakespeare, William. *Hamlet*, *The Tempest*

Shank, Ted. *American Alternative Theatre*

Shaw, Bernard. *Pygmalion*

Shepard, Sam. *Fool for Love*, *True West*

Sills, Paul. *Story Theatre*

Simon, Neil. *The Odd Couple*

Sondheim, Steven and James Lapine. *Into the Woods*

Sondheim, Steven and John Weidman. *Assassins*

Sophocles. *Oedipus Rex*

Spolin, Viola. *Improvisation for the Theatre*

Terkel, Studs. *Working*

Terry, Megan. *Comings and Goings*

Veiller, Bayard. *The Thirteenth Chair*

Williams, Tennessee. *A Streetcar Named Desire*, *The Glass Menagerie*